Nature Walks
& Sunday Drives
'Round Edmonton

To Jack & Luke
May we Have
Many Nature
Walks.
Love Mommy &
Daddy April 01

Henry Saley

Harry Stelfox

Dave Ealey

Edmonton
Natural History
Club

ENVIRONMENTAL PROTECTION

The Publisher:
   Edmonton Natural History Club
   Box 1582
   Edmonton, Alberta T5J 2N9

Canadian Cataloguing in Publication Data
   Saley, Henry, 1953-.
   Nature Walks & Sunday Drives 'Round Edmonton
   ISBN #0-9698507-1-9 (pbk.)

Second Printing, 1999

Design: Gigi Meade
Layout: Douglas Boratynec and Judy Fushtey
Cover illustration: Lorna Bennett
Black-and-white illustrations: Gary Ross
Cartography: Trevor Wiens
Printing: DeJong Printing Ltd., Edmonton, Alberta

Preface

BY JOY AND CAM FINLAY

Having been explorers of nature in and around Edmonton for nearly 40 years, we are delighted to see so many familiar places featured in this first guide to nature-viewing sites in the Edmonton region. We never cease to marvel at the unique aspects of landforms, the character of wildlife communities and the richness of seasons that typify each special place. And no matter how often we go to each place, there is always something we've never seen before. It takes a book like this to help identify and describe the valuable natural areas within and close to our ever-growing urban centre. It takes a book like this to also demonstrate that, although nature may be all around us, space must be saved for the natural world to be sustained. As a result of cumulative efforts by individuals and organizations, natural areas have begun to be protected.

In Elk Island National Park, a cross-country skier can view the largest land mammal in North America. And for the record, the smallest land mammal in North America is also found there. In between the largest wood bison and the smallest pygmy shrew, you can find moose, elk and deer, all at home in the only national park with a fence around it.

Besides being the chickadee capital of the world, according to annual bird counts, Edmonton has one of the highest concentrations of black-billed magpies. Merlins, which occupy the magpies' abandoned twig nests, thrive here because of the abundance of waxwings, which in turn thrive on all the berries of mountain ashes that have been planted in city yards and have spread into the river valley. For all things there is a reason; the cause-and-effect connections between the sun, rain, us, you, plants, animals and all of nature just keep us exploring in thought long after we have walked a trail.

The publication of this guidebook is a happy event, for it further confirms a value we hold of having natural places for all to enjoy. Even more, we are thankful that protected natural places are there to be featured in a book. It is proof that, as a society, we are starting to become caring stewards of the natural treasures in our environment, for our own sake and for the sake of nature too.

Whether wandering in a poplar bush, skiing through spruce woods, walking on a boardwalk in a muskeg, or paddling around a big slough or lake, enjoy!

*Black-Capped
Chickadee*

Corporate Sponsors

The production of this guide has been assisted by the generous financial support of our corporate sponsors as shown below.

Alberta Sport, Recreation, Parks and Wildlife Foundation: supporting the development of parks; recreation programs and services; and the management, conservation and preservation of fish and wildlife.

Elk Island National Park: a wilderness retreat harboring diverse flora and fauna of the transitional aspen parkland–managed by Parks Canada and less than an hour's drive from the City of Edmonton.

Federation of Alberta Naturalists: the voice of Alberta naturalists–promoting the enjoyment, study and conservation of Alberta's natural history.

Canada Trust—Friends of the Environment Foundation: bringing people together in ways that contribute to the overall health of the Canadian environment.

Interprovincial Pipe Line Inc. – Community Based Environmental Initiative Program: helping local groups to take action on their commitment to environmental protection, conservation and public awareness.

Shell Canada Limited – Shell Environmental Fund: an annual program to help individuals and small groups make a positive contribution to our environment.

$\mathcal{C}$ontents

Page

Introduction 1
    Take a Nature Break 1
    Who Can Use This Guide? 1
    Tips for Watching Wildlife With Respect 2
    How to Use This Guide 3

Edmonton Area Nature Almanac 4

City of Edmonton Viewing Sites 5
    Edmonton River Valley Parks 6
    John Janzen Nature Centre 8
    Whitemud Ravine 8
    William Hawrelak Park 10
    Victoria Park 10
    Kinsmen Park 11
    Mill Creek Park 12
    Gold Bar Park 13

West of Edmonton Viewing Sites 14
    Battle Lake (Alberta 4-H Centre) 16
    Chickakoo Lake Recreation Area 18
    Clifford E. Lee Nature Sanctuary 20
    Coyote Lake Nature Sanctuary 22
    Devonian Botanic Garden (University of Alberta) .. 24
    Hasse Lake Provincial Park 26
    Red Willow Park (St. Albert) 28
    Wabamun Lake 30
    Wagner Natural Area 32

East of Edmonton Viewing Sites 34
    Beaverhill Lake (Tofield) 36
    Blackfoot Recreation Area 38
    Dow Wildlife Greenbelt Viewing Area 40
    Elk Island National Park 42
    Halfmoon Lake Natural Area 44
    Miquelon Lake Provincial Park 46
    Sherwood Park Natural Area 48
    Strathcona Wilderness Centre 50
    Telford Lake (Leduc) 52

	Page
Wabamun Lake - Lac Ste. Anne Auto Tour	54
Cooking Lake Moraine Auto Tour	58
Gwynne Outlet Auto Tour	62
Sources for Further Information	66
Agency and Organization Contacts	66
Editor's Choice of References	67

Acknowledgements

This book is the result of a cooperative effort involving a large number of committed individuals from several naturalist and nongovernment organizations, as well as from municipal, provincial and federal government agencies. This cooperative effort has been spearheaded and coordinated by the two primary project sponsors: the Edmonton Natural History Club and Alberta Environmental Protection (Natural Resources Service).

Contributors provided advice, attended planning meetings, reviewed draft materials and field-checked viewing sites and auto tour routes—often on their own time and at their own expense. I would particularly like to acknowledge the following individuals who were substantively involved in several, if not all, phases of the project from initial planning to final printing: John Acorn, Pat and Dick Clayton, Patsy Cotterill, Dave Ealey and John Folinsbee. In addition, the following individuals were actively involved in the project in one way or another, many in a volunteer capacity.

Elisabeth Beaubien	Roger Bryan	Ross Chapman
Murray Christman	Doug Culbert	Patti Danos
Peter Demulder	Richard DeSmet	Loney Dickson
Dave Doze	Jean Funk	Alice Hendry
Alan Hingston	Geoff Holroyd	Doris Hopkins
Eric Hopkins	Derek Johnson	Jackie Kallal
Bob Lane	Jim Lange	Gerry Lunn
Ray Makowecki	Andy McCracken	Sandy Myers
Wayne Nordstrom	Doug Nothstein	Sandra Opdenkamp
Claire Radke	Marg Reine	Bill Reynolds
Martin Sawdon	Manny Schmidt	Carol Smith
Brad Stelfox	Randy Strocki	Tom Sutherland
Bruce Turner	Judy Vance	Cindy Verbeek
Dennis Verbeek	Dave Westworth	Ed Whitelock

Claire Radke and David Doyle were contracted as the primary researchers and compilers of background information on viewing sites and auto tour routes. Henry Saley (Orchis Communications Design) was contracted to undertake the principal writing. Dave Ealey of Alberta Environmental Protection served also as the editor-in-chief.

This book was produced on a lean, 1990s-style budget. In addition to the initial funding commitments

Northern Saw-whet Owl

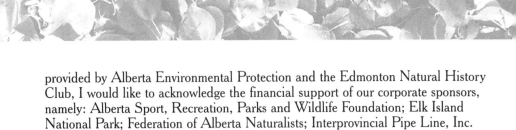

provided by Alberta Environmental Protection and the Edmonton Natural History Club, I would like to acknowledge the financial support of our corporate sponsors, namely: Alberta Sport, Recreation, Parks and Wildlife Foundation; Elk Island National Park; Federation of Alberta Naturalists; Interprovincial Pipe Line, Inc. (Community Based Environmental Initiative Program); and Shell Canada Limited (Shell Environmental Fund).

Harry Stelfox
Project Manager

Symbols Legend

FACILITIES AND ACTIVITIES

Boat Launch		Observation Platform/Viewpoint	
Brochure/Checklists		Picnic/Day Use	
Canoe Launch		Picnic Shelter	
Cycling		Self-guided Trail	
Entry Fee		Swimming	
Fishing		Tent Camping	
Guided Tour		Toilets	
Hiking/Walking Trail		Trail Riding	
Interpretive Displays/Programs		Wheelchair Accessible*	
		X-Country Skiing	

*Wheelchair accessibility is indicated only for those sites that have been designated as such by the responsible site management authority. Access for parking and washrooms should be good, but access to the trail system may be variable and localized. Phone the appropriate site information contact for further details.

Introduction

Take a Nature Break

Explore over 25 of the best watchable wildlife spots in and around Edmonton. It's a great way to be active, spend time with family and friends and leave behind everyday stresses. The more you experience the natural world, the more you'll get hooked on discovering new sights. This guide covers the Edmonton viewing region, as outlined in the following map.

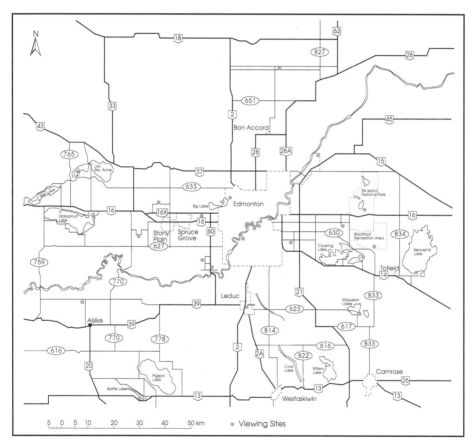

Who Can Use This Guide?

Whether you're young, or a senior, in a group or on your own, you'll find this guide a good start to finding the animals, plants and landscapes that make up Edmonton and the surrounding area.

Most sites (except some stops on the auto tours) have well-marked access, good parking and developed trails.

Tips for Watching Wildlife With Respect

FOR BEST SUMMER VIEWING SUCCESS, VISIT DURING MORNINGS OR EARLY EVENINGS.

Midday is a time when most wildlife are resting or just staying out of the heat. However, if that's the most convenient time for you, there are still some terrific things to be seen. Wildflowers and butterflies are at their best during midday and some animals are active from dawn to dusk.

MOVE SLOWLY AND QUIETLY.

Animals are always aware of potential danger. They assume that you intend to make a meal of them. Try sitting quietly on a bench or log for several minutes. The surrounding wildlife will become more accustomed to your presence and may then go about their normal activities.

STAY ON DEVELOPED TRAILS AS MUCH AS POSSIBLE.

Trails are for trampling on—the undergrowth is not. Healthy undergrowth is critical for animal food and shelter. Animals adapt to a regular flow of people along a trail, but too many people in unexpected places may cause them to move out of an area.

KEEP A RESPECTFUL DISTANCE.

If the animal stays alert to your presence, you are too close. Your respect and common sense can ensure that new young are raised and not abandoned. Some animals, like pelicans, may never return if disturbed too often.

BRING BINOCULARS AND FIELD GUIDES.

You can certainly enjoy yourself with minimal equipment. However, binoculars will give you a better view of those elusive animals on a lake, high in a tree or across a wide meadow. Field guides will help you to identify the plants and animals. Suggested resources are listed at the end of each site description and at the back of this guide.

GO A STEP FURTHER THAN JUST SPOTTING AND IDENTIFYING.

If you can identify what you see, that's rewarding. To get even more enjoyment, watch the behaviour of birds and other wildlife. You'll soon know not just what they look like and what their name is, but where they are commonly found, what they eat, how they move and other interesting things about the way they live.

WATCH AND LISTEN FOR ANIMAL SIGNS.

Finding telltale signs of animal activity can be as rewarding as seeing the animals themselves. Look for trails, nests, tracks, browse (chewed plants),

tunnels in wood, burrows and droppings. Animal droppings are surprisingly easy to identify. Listen for the territorial and breeding calls of birds, frogs and other wildlife, especially at springtime.

CARRY A NOTEBOOK TO RECORD YOUR DISCOVERIES.

You'll be amazed at how a few notes here and there will add up to a fine record of your outdoor adventures. Try keeping a journal of your sightings throughout the year, including dates, locations and interesting behaviours. Your notes may interest other naturalists, biologists and site managers.

How to Use This Guide

Viewing Sites

1. Choose a site from the Table of Contents and check the overview map at the beginning of the section that incorporates the site.

2. Each site description introduces a few commonly seen features and some special ones. Keep in mind that this description is only a small sample of what each site has to offer. Detailed site maps and other brochures, available at most sites, will give you more information. Refer also to "Suggested guides for more discovery" at the end of each site description.

3. Symbols beside each site map indicate facilities that are available and activities that are supported. Refer to the symbols legend on page viii.

4. "Things to do" focuses on those activities that are friendly to the environment and compatible with wildlife viewing. Some sites have various facilities for recreation. Call the contact number for more information.

Auto Tours

Auto tours provide a self-guiding route by which you can visit a few viewing sites and other points of interest on a one-day outing. Interesting features and stops are pointed out along the way.

1. Choose an auto tour from the Table of Contents.

2. Review the overview map at the beginning of each tour description.

3. The tours give choices for stopping at several sites along the way. Based on the time you wish to spend, choose the sites that are right for you. You can certainly plan to do the tours more than once, stopping at different sites each trip. We suggest taking along an up-to-date road map or, better still, an access map at a scale of 1:250 000 (available from Maps Alberta outlets).

Edmonton Area
NATURE ALMANAC

January	Snowy owls are often seen in the countryside, perching on power poles and fence posts–keeping a watchful eye for mice and voles.
February	Listen for the yodelling and yipping of coyotes on a clear night–they become more vocal during their breeding season.
March	Black-capped chickadees begin to excavate nest cavities and the first crows return–sure signs of spring.
April	Attend the Snow Goose Festival at Beaverhill Lake to view thousands of geese: snows, Canadas and greater white-fronts.
May	Listen to wood frogs "quacking" their spring breeding calls from flooded ditches and marshy areas.
June	A profusion of white blossoms cover choke cherry, pin cherry and saskatoon shrubs in the river valley and adjacent ravines.
July	This month is butterfly season and the river valley is a-flutter with sulphurs, blues, anglewings, and skippers. To learn more, join the butterfly count at the John Janzen Nature Centre.
August	The southern migration of shorebirds and warblers peaks, as does the bird banding activity at the Beaverhill Bird Observatory.
September	The smell of ripened high-bush cranberry in aspen woods is a sure sign of fall–also a good time to search out various types of mushrooms.
October	Large flocks of ducks and geese can be seen making flights to and from water bodies and grain fields in preparation for the fall migration.
November	Project Feeder Watch begins for those who wish to monitor their bird feeders on a regular basis and report their observations– contact the John Janzen Nature Centre for more details.
December	Join the Edmonton Christmas Bird Count by contacting the John Janzen Nature Centre–a good time for a family outing and to meet other naturalists.

City of Edmonton
VIEWING SITES

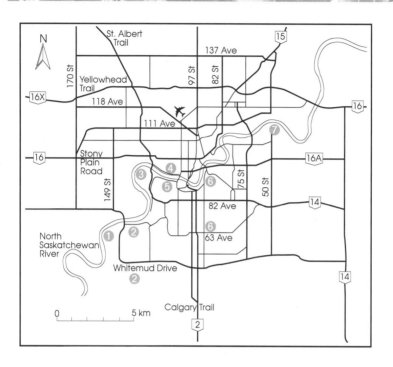

Site Name	Special Features	Page
❶ John Janzen Nature Centre	Richardson's ground squirrels, red-winged blackbirds, pond study, nature displays and programs	8
❷ Whitemud Ravine	white spruce, red squirrels, aspen forest, snowshoe hares, coyotes, white-tailed deer, mule deer, balsam poplar, river alder, beaver	8
❸ William Hawrelak Park	ducks, black-capped chickadees, merlins, woodpeckers, nuthatches	10
❹ Victoria Park	grassland and flowering native shrubs, song sparrows, ring-necked pheasants	10
❺ Kinsmen Park	poplar and spruce woods, northern orioles, bunchberry, dogwood	11
❻ Mill Creek Park	waxwings, merlins, nuthatches	12
❼ Gold Bar Park	winter waterfowl, blue jays, butterflies	13

Edmonton River Valley Parks

In the early days of Edmonton's history, the city leaders identified the river valley and adjacent ravines for preservation. Today, the park system extends for about 32 km through the centre of the city. The main hiking trails follow the river valley with secondary trails extending into numerous connecting ravines. Trails link park areas throughout the city to create one of the largest urban green belts in North America. Though previously disturbed by settlement, mining and lumbering, the river valley is slowly returning to a natural state and becoming valuable parkland for wildlife and man.

Special features

Spring and fall are great times to watch for thousands of birds that use the river valley as a **migration corridor**. **Bald eagles**, which are more like scavengers than predators, patrol the river for dead fish washed onshore. **Ring-billed gulls**, returning from as far as Mexico, are very noticeable along the riverbanks in late March. **Flycatchers, thrushes, vireos** and **warblers** pass through in large numbers during mid-May. Some of them stay to nest in the valley. These songbirds begin heading south in August. **Sandhill cranes** fly noisily overhead in September, on their way to California and farther south.

Great horned owls begin nesting as early as February in the ravines. By the time spring leaves begin unfolding in early May, the young owls are departing nests to explore their nearby world.

Peregrine falcons nest on the AGT Toll Building in the centre of Edmonton at 100 Street and 102 Avenue and also the Clinical Sciences Building beside the Mackenzie Health Sciences Centre (U of A campus). The best viewing for the AGT site is from the east side, at the Centennial Library. In 1993 and 1994, Edmonton had three pairs of breeding peregrines, more than any other Canadian city.

The **black-billed magpie** is a handsome and common bird in Edmonton. A world record (3219 magpies) was tallied during the city's 1988 Christmas Bird Count. This year-round resident prefers to live in areas settled by man. It scavenges road kills and feeds on worms, grasshoppers, and many insects that we consider harmful.

Black-capped chickadees also occur in record numbers in Edmonton. They are dependable companions on any outing. If you're patient, you might entice them to take sunflower seeds right out of your outstretched hand. In spring, listen for their mating song: a sweetly melancholy "here, sweetie."

Things to do

- check into educational and recreational programs available for families, birthday parties, conventions and other groups

- take part in a special event organized by a parks leader

- enroll your children in a spring or summer day camp

- visit one of the interpretive facilities: John Janzen Nature Centre, Fort Edmonton Park, Provincial Museum, Valley Zoo, John Walter Museum

- angle for fish along the river; catch and release is recommended

- bicycle, jog or picnic along the Capital City Park trails

- join with members of the Edmonton Bird Club or the Edmonton Natural History Club to participate in Christmas Bird Counts, May Species Counts and field trips

- pick up brochures at the River Valley Outdoor Centre for cross-country ski trails, fishing and cycling

For more information, contact:

River Valley Outdoor Centre: 496-7275
Nature Information Line (John Janzen Nature Centre): 496-2910
Northern Alberta Bird Hotline number: 433-BIRD

Suggested guides for more discovery

Cycle Edmonton - Map, Information and Trail Guide, City of Edmonton, 1993.

Cross Country Ski Edmonton - General Information and Ski Area Maps, City of Edmonton.

*Urban Fishing Brochure.*1988. City of Edmonton.

Edmonton Naturalist. Journal of the Edmonton Natural History Club published three times a year.

Walking Guides to Mill Creek Ravine and Whitemud Ravine Nature Reserve. Edmonton Natural History Club, Box 1582, Edmonton, Alberta T5J 2N9.

John Janzen Nature Centre

Special features

Knowledgeable staff, public events, live animal displays and a self-guiding trail make this facility a logical place to start experiencing nature in the city. **Richardson's ground squirrels** scurry across the open grass as you approach the centre. In late summer, they collect seeds to store in underground chambers, but since they are winter hibernators, they may not use this food until spring. A small pond and a marsh, created adjacent to the nature centre, attract easily spotted **ducks, songbirds** and **wood frogs**. Ask at the nature centre for small nets and field guides for catching and identifying "minibeasts" from the pond waters. Always return your catch to the pond. Beginning behind the centre, trail signs tell you about the wildlife discoveries of the fictitious Woods family as they explore the **aspen, birch** and **poplar forests** in the river valley.

Richardson's Ground Squirrel

Getting there

Exit from Whitemud Drive to Fox Drive and watch for the directional signs to Fort Edmonton Park and the John Janzen Nature Centre.

Whitemud Ravine

Whitemud Ravine gives a feeling of wilderness in the city. This picturesque ravine carves up to 60 m deep from the southwest edge of the city through to the river valley. The ravine features a small meandering creek and contains the highest diversity of plants and animals in the city. Nine kilometres of trails lead you through changing scenes of forests, open fields and bottomlands along the creek.

Special features

White spruce forests offer a cool and protected shelter for many animals. Up in the trees, **red squirrels** chatter from a safe distance. They are agitated by your intrusion into their territory. Look for their mossy summer nests built high in a spruce tree and for discarded cone scales that form piles, called middens, on the ground. In the winter, their tracks are the ones that always lead from tree to tree. During really cold days, they stay warm in underground dens.

Red Squirrel

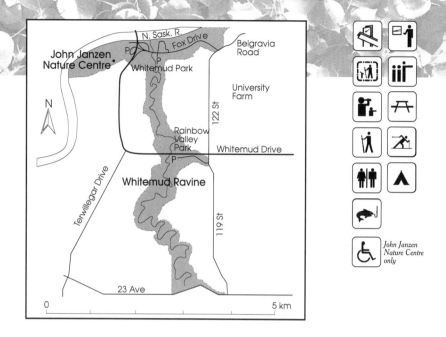

Aspen forests permit light to filter through their leaves, allowing a lush growth of wildflowers and shrubs. The **snowshoe hare** snips away this undergrowth along its travel highways. These runways are especially noticeable in winter. Look closely at hare tracks and note the huge size difference between the front and hind feet. Where a hare has been resting or feeding, you'll find tan-coloured droppings (bunny buttons) left behind.

In soft, moist areas of ground, you'll see the tracks of **white-tailed** and **mule deer**. Stay quiet when exploring the ravine in the early morning or at dusk, and you'll have a good chance of seeing these graceful animals feeding along the forest edge. In the winter, they munch the tender twigs of shrubs such as **red-osier dogwood** and **willows**.

Balsam poplar and **river alder** are common along the creek because they grow so well in wet soil. In the fall, look for large clusters of freshly cut twigs and branches in the water. **Beaver** store these food caches to survive the winter. A beaver can cut through a good-sized poplar in a matter of 20 minutes, if uninterrupted. To make up for continual wear, its strong "buck" teeth (incisors) grow continuously. Grassy meadows have likely been cleared of trees by beaver.

Getting there

Exit from Fox Drive to Keillor Road, drive around the picnic area and back under the bridge over Whitemud Creek, *or*

Exit from Whitemud Freeway at 122 Street heading south and take access road to Rainbow Valley Park.

William Hawrelak Park

Would you believe that more dollars are spent worldwide on sand and gravel than on gold, platinum or diamonds? Not surprisingly then, sand and gravel are Alberta's most valuable mineral resources, next to oil! Hawrelak Park is situated on a former extraction site that supplied sand and gravel for building bridges, roads, airports and other such city projects, from the early 1900s on. This extraction site was reclaimed as a park with grassy expanses, trees and a pond. **Waterfowl** offer a great opportunity for **photography** in this area because they are unusually tame from being fed by people. However, feeding wildlife may do some harm by upsetting their normal diet. The man-made lake and its islands attract **Canada geese, mallards** and **common goldeneyes.**

Getting there

Exit from Groat Road, on south side of the river and follow signs to William Hawrelak Park.

Mallard

Victoria Park

If you live or work near the city centre, take a nature break in the river valley. Grassland, shrubs and patchy tree cover are typical of the sunny north side of the river valley. The slopes face south and receive direct sunlight, which creates a warm, dry environment. Flowering shrubs such as **choke cherry, saskatoon** and **pin cherry** attract a colourful and musical collection of songbirds. One of the first birds to arrive here in the spring is the lively **song sparrow**. It builds a nest on the ground or in a shrub. Throughout the summer, you'll find it scratching the ground for weed seeds.

Getting there

Trails begin at the top of the riverbank at Ezio Faraone Park adjacent the High Level Bridge or down a stairway at Le Marchand Mansion at 116th St. and 100th Ave. Free parking is available at Victoria Park just off the River Valley Road in the valley bottom.

Choke Cherry

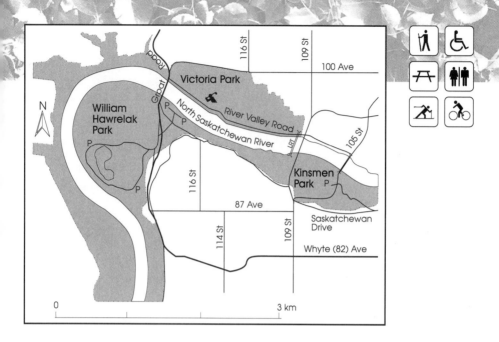

Kinsmen Park

Wooded stands of balsam poplar mixed with spruce are typical of the south side of the river, where the environment of these north-facing banks is cool and moist. The tree cover is a good buffer against the noise from inner city traffic. Look for a flash of orange and black in the tops of poplar trees as **northern orioles** scour the branches for caterpillars and other insects. **Bunchberries** decorate the forest floor with their large white flower clusters in early summer. If you look closely, you'll see that the white "petals" are actually bracts (a type of leaf), which surround numerous tiny, white flowers clustered in the middle. The flowers develop into bright red berries in late summer.

Bunchberry

Getting there

Park at the Kinsmen Sports Centre by the 105th St. bridge (east side of site) or at Emily Murphy Park just east of the Groat Road bridge (west end of site). Trails begin from the top of the valley at the south end of the High Level Bridge and also from Saskatchewan Drive just above the LRT tunnel to the university. A pedestrian/cycle path under the LRT bridge lets you cross the river to Victoria Park.

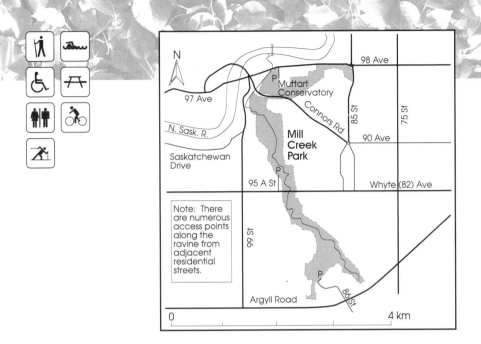

Mill Creek Park

Mixed forests of white spruce, aspen, balsam poplar and birch attract a variety of birds, including **blue jays**, **Bohemian waxwings** and **brown creepers**.

Bohemian waxwings feed on the abundant fruit trees planted in the city, especially the bright orange berries of the mountain ash. More than 16 000 waxwings have been counted during some winters! **Merlins** are able to stay in the city year-round by feeding on overwintering waxwings and resident house sparrows. These small but feisty falcons raise their young in old magpie nests. More than 50 nesting pairs have been seen in the city—the highest known breeding population of any city in the world.

Getting there

Parking is available by the swimming pool at 95A St. north of 82nd Ave., at Muttart Conservatory in the main river valley and by the Velodrome near 86 St. and Argyll Road.

Merlin

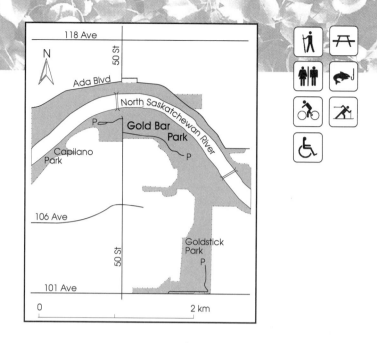

Gold Bar Park

Warm water discharged from the Rossdale power-generating plant keeps the river from freezing, making this a good birdwatching spot year-round. Hundreds of ducks, mostly **mallard** and **common goldeneye,** are spotted on the open water of the river during the annual Christmas Bird Count.

This park was named for the gravel bars at the mouth of Gold Bar Creek, where early miners panned for gold. From mid-May to July, many butterflies, including the **Canadian tiger swallowtail**, patrol the edges of Gold Bar Creek looking for mates. **Blue jays** frequent the park throughout the year. You may be puzzled by the origin of a very unusual bird call, only to find that the blue jay has fooled you again with a sound from its wide repertoire.

Common Goldeneye

Getting there

Parking is reached from 50th Street on the south side of the river.

West of Edmonton

VIEWING SITES

Site Name	Distance from Edmonton City Centre	Special Features	Page
❶ Battle Lake (Alberta 4-H Centre)	108 km SW	glacial drainage channel, ravines, fern glade, bald eagles, common loons, tree swallows, red-necked grebes, porcupines	16
❷ Chickakoo Lake Recreation Area	63 km W	pitted delta, common loons, puddle ducks, diving ducks, beaver, muskrats, willow groves, mourning cloak butterflies	18
❸ Clifford E. Lee Nature Sanctuary	33 km SW	marsh wrens, red-winged and yellow-headed blackbirds, blue darner dragonflies, black terns, water milfoil, sand dunes, tiger beetles	20
❹ Coyote Lake Nature Sanctuary	94 km SW	common loons, great blue herons, marsh marigolds, cotton grass, common red paintbrush, western wood lilies	22
❺ Devonian Botanic Garden (University of Alberta)	33 km SW	Plants of Alberta and Native Peoples' Garden, tamarack fen, boreal chickadees, hairy woodpeckers, horsetail, wild black currant	24
❻ Hasse Lake Provincial Park	40 km W	brook sticklebacks, ruffed grouse, ruddy ducks, American coots, northern pocket gophers	26
❼ Red Willow Park (St. Albert)	14 km NW	mink, riverside trails, tiger salamanders, wood frogs, northern pintails, ermine, warbling vireos	28
❽ Wabamun Lake	65 km W	ospreys, common terns, belted kingfishers, great blue herons, pike, perch, white suckers, whitefish, bald eagles, gyrfalcons, winter waterfowl	30
❾ Wagner Natural Area	22 km W	carnivorous plants, wood frogs, marl ponds, stonewort, brown moss, marsh marigolds, bog violets, western wood lilies, round-leaved orchids	32

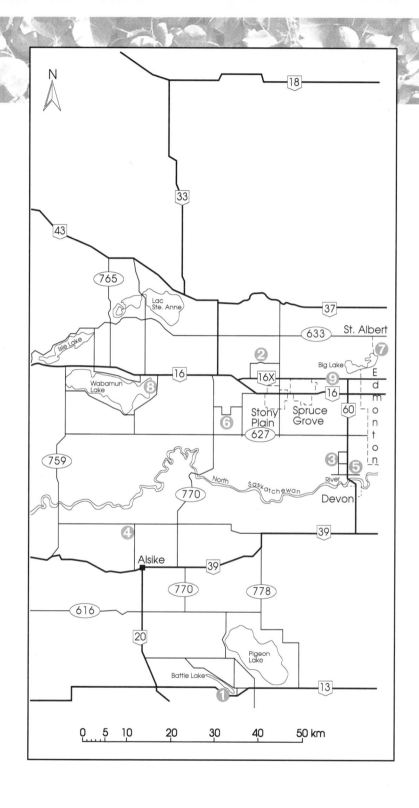

N

18

33

43

765

Lac
Ste. Anne

Isle Lake

37

633   St. Albert

2

16X   Big Lake   7

Wabamun
Lake   8   16   9   E
d
16   m
o
60   n
Stony   Spruce   t
Plain   Grove   o
6   n
627

759   3
5

North   Saskatchewan   River
770   Devon

4   39

Alsike
39

770   778

616

20

Pigeon
Lake

Battle Lake   1   13

0   5   10   20   30   40   50 km

Battle Lake

Location: 108 km southwest of Edmonton city centre
Suggested first-time viewing: 1.5 hours to walk Fern Valley Trail and Porcupine Trail

This privately owned site is operated by the Alberta 4-H Foundation. Visitors are welcome, but be sure to check in with the site managers upon your arrival to let them know of your presence and interests.

Around 10 000 years ago, in this very spot, melting glaciers unleashed a torrent of water that carved a deep river valley. Today, the valley contains a long, deep and narrow lake–the headwaters of the Battle River. A hiking trail begins on the scenic edge of the valley, then drops suddenly into a cavernous ravine containing a lush forest of ferns and towering balsam poplars.

Special features

During a period of thousands of years, the **ravine** was gouged by a creek that now meanders into the lake. During spring runoff and summer floods, water gushes downstream with enough force to carry fallen trees and a great deal of sand, gravel and silt. Where the creek enters the lake, the flowing water suddenly slows and the suspended dirt finally settles. Over the years, the build-up of dirt has created a large area of fertile soil–a delta–on which the ferns and balsam poplars grow.

The **fern glade** is truly impressive. By midsummer, **ostrich ferns** stand over a metre tall. In the centre of the clumps of fronds are shorter, stiff, dark green leaves that become brown or blackish by late summer–these are the fertile fronds. They bear clusters of spore cases on the rolled-under leaf margins. Each cluster releases thousands of spores, some of which will land in suitable conditions to grow a new fern plant.

Bald Eagle

A cool, narrow gully exposes **65-million-year-old bedrock** of sandstone and shale. This bedrock underlies the entire Battle Lake area. At the delta formed downstream of this gully, you get a terrific view of the lake. **Bald eagles** nest along the shore, but you're more likely to see **common loons, red-necked grebes** or **tree swallows**. With a sharp eye, you may spot an **osprey, great blue heron** or **belted kingfisher**, each with a unique talent for catching fish.

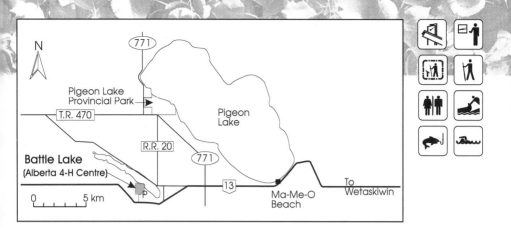

Porcupine

On the Porcupine Trail, your feet will sink into the mossy floor of the spruce forest. Here, **porcupines** have been busy girdling the bark from trees, with some trunks stripped clean. Look also for the trimmed twigs on red-osier dogwood and willow shrubs; these twigs are not pruned by shears but by the teeth of **deer** and **moose**.

Things to do

- launch a canoe to explore more of this 7-km long lake
- hunt for different colours and textures of rocks along the streams (please leave the rocks for others to enjoy)
- book facilities and services for a group: dormitory, lodge with dining facilities and games room, archery, canoeing, baseball, volleyball, backcountry camping, fire circle, environmental appreciation programs and the Grant MacEwan Environmental Centre

For more information, contact:

Site Managers, Vern and Shirley Schneider, Alberta 4-H Centre, Battle Lake 682-2153

Suggested guides for more discovery

Exploring the Trails. 1994. Henry Saley, 4-H Foundation of Alberta, Edmonton. (available at site)

Chickakoo Lake
RECREATION AREA

Location: 63 km west of Edmonton city centre
Suggested first-time viewing: Pick up the Eco Trail brochure and take 1 hour to discover the natural features along Indian Ridge Trail

Chickakoo Lake is part of the Glory Hills, a landscape created thousands of years ago when rivers from melting glaciers deposited large amounts of sand and silt. Chunks of glacial ice were buried in this "delta," leaving pits when the ice chunks melted. This landscape is called a pitted delta, with Chickakoo Lake occupying one of the pits. Today, the area is a 194-ha wildlife sanctuary of forest, lake and pond. The wooded trails follow the shoreline, giving a good view of lakeshore wildlife and plants.

Special features

Common loons nest on Chickakoo Lake, but since they need a large breeding territory, you are likely to see only one pair. You can distinguish them from ducks by their sharply pointed bill and larger, longer body. The call of the loon is a sound you never forget.

Ducks seen on the lakes and ponds are of two groups. Try to identify them:

The **dabbling ducks**, such as mallard and northern pintail, tip up to feed, mooning any passersby. They take straight off from the water's surface when alarmed and usually swim with their tail held well above the water.

The **diving ducks**, such as bufflehead and common goldeneye, dive completely underwater to feed. They run along the surface of the water for a distance before lifting off and swim with their tails held close to the water.

Beaver are a symbol for Chickakoo Lake since they seem to be active everywhere. Their lodges, built mostly with aspen branches, each take about a month to build and are used for many years. Other signs are felled trees, stumps and branches with large teeth marks. A natural lumberman, a beaver can fell over 200 trees a year. Not bad for one set of teeth. Beaver incisors are continually growing to make up for the wear. A swimming **muskrat** is sometimes mistaken for a beaver. To tell them apart, remember that the muskrat is smaller and has a snake-like tail wriggling at the water's surface.

Beaver

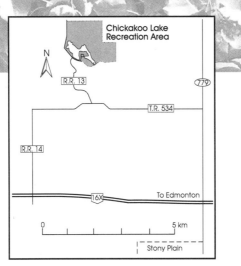

Willow groves are a common sight at the lake edge. In the spring, look for the fuzzy catkins (flowers). They often burst out before the leaves do, which lets the wind blow the pollen about and more effectively fertilize the female flowers. If that doesn't work, insects such as **mourning cloak butterflies** transfer pollen from flower to flower as they search for nectar.

Lesser Scaup

Things to do

- ride a mountain bike or hike the 14 km of maintained trails
- fish for brook trout (stocked annually)
- skate on the lake or cross-country ski during winter

For more information, contact:

The County of Parkland, Transportation and Utilities   963-8448

Suggested guides for more discovery

Chickakoo Lake Eco Trail, A Self-guided Interpretive Tour, County of Parkland, Parks and Recreation Department.

Winter Environment Study Programs, County of Parkland, Parks and Recreation Department.

Location: 33 km southwest of Edmonton city centre
Suggested first-time viewing: 1.5 hours to hike the boardwalk

Watch how the assortment of plants changes completely as you move from aspen woods to marsh, then to meadow and finally to the sandy soils of a pine forest. This variety of habitat attracts a diverse and abundant wildlife community that is remarkably lush for such a compact site. The boardwalk makes for terrific viewing of the marsh world—a habitat that teems with animals and vegetation.

Special features

Look for these birds along the boardwalk that weaves through the marsh:

Marsh wrens have a distinctive musical rattle. Look for their ball-shaped nests woven into the stems of cattails up to a metre above the water.

Red-winged and **yellow-headed blackbirds** build their cup-shaped nests in much the same way. In spring, listen for the red-winged males belting out "O-ka-ree-a" as they sway precariously on top of a cattail. Compared to the bright colours of the males, the females might be considered boring to look at. However, their streaked, dark colours blend in very well with their surroundings: a handy feature when they sit on a nest.

Blue darner dragonflies, among the largest insects in Alberta, feed on mosquitoes and other flying insects. Be nice to them. A single dragonfly can wolf down 133 mosquitos a day.

Yellow-headed Blackbird

Black terns skim over the open water of the marsh. Watching them, you would think they spent their entire lives in the air! This tern snaps up insects as it flies.

Look into the clear water in early spring to see bright-green plant balls lying on the bottom. These are the winter buds of **water milfoil**, a feathery aquatic plant. The buds soon sprout, roots form and a new season's growth begins.

Sand dunes make up the soil that lies under your feet as you explore the higher land around the marsh. About 10 000 years ago, a gigantic lake covered the Edmonton area, its water held in place by huge glaciers. As the glaciers melted, the lake drained away, leaving expanses of muddy sand and silt. Strong winds blew much of this dirt to far off places, but the heavy sand was deposited here, where it is now called the Devon Sandhills. (Pine Knoll Trail)

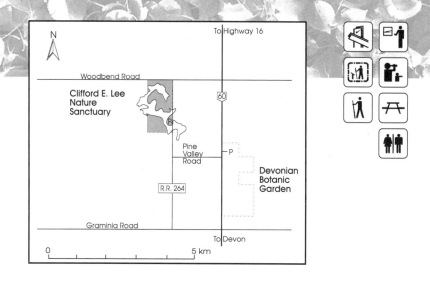

Look for the **tiger beetle** scurrying away as you approach. If you get too close, it will suddenly fly up and then land some distance away. As a larva, this predator is ferocious for its size and waits in tiny pits in the sand for its prey to come along. When an insect approaches or falls into the pit, the larva grabs it with powerful jaws. (Meadow Trail, exposed sandy areas)

Things to do

- join an informal walk of the trails with a naturalist group
- take a school or youth group for pond study along the boardwalk

For more information, contact:

Alberta Fish and Wildlife, Natural Resources Service, Stony Plain 963-6131

Wild Strawberries

This site is owned by the Canadian Nature Federation and managed by a local volunteer group, the Clifford E. Lee Nature Sanctuary Management Committee, 51306 Range Road 264, Spruce Grove, Alberta T7Y 1E7.

Suggested guides for more discovery

Local volunteers have developed a series of brochure guides (available on site) for interpreting the pond life, waterfowl, insects and other features.

Coyote Lake

NATURE SANCTUARY

Location: 94 km southwest of Edmonton city centre via Leduc

Suggested first-time viewing: 1 hour to hike from Hopkins' House to the lake boardwalk and around the first meadow

The owners of the Coyote Lake Nature Sanctuary welcome visitors who wish to enjoy the natural wonders of their site. Three ecological zones meet in this area: boreal forest, aspen parkland and foothills. Over 150 species each of birds and wildflowers are attracted to this diverse mix of vegetation. In just a few kilometres of trails, you'll get a wonderful taste of that diversity. Begin by enjoying the views from around Hopkins' House. A boardwalk takes you over the marshy shoreline to get a full view of the lake.

Special features

Loons nesting on Coyote Lake are in easy view of the main house. It'll bring a smile to your face when you see the young fluffy loon chicks riding on their parents' backs (June-July). Visiting loons sometimes join in a social ritual with the nesting pair. With much yodeling, they form a ring, dive into the water, surface about 8 m away and then regroup to repeat their loon square dance. (mornings in June and July, viewing platforms in first meadow and at end of boardwalk leading from Hopkins' House)

Common Loon

Great blue herons commonly feed at this lake. They are probably yearlings (hatched the previous summer) from a nearby nesting colony. Yearlings don't nest and are not well tolerated by nesting birds. These immatures must find their own feeding habitat and this lake seems to fill the bill. (early evenings)

Moose

Moose, deer and **wapiti** (elk) are attracted to a natural mineral lick at Saltlick Viewpoint. After passing through some dense bush, the trail opens on a rise overlooking a grassy bowl. Wildlife tracks are everywhere on the wet ground of this scenic and wild place. Make a visit at dawn or dusk for a fine chance of seeing moose, deer or elk. (Saltlick Viewpoint and Moose Meadow)

You'll find wildflowers in each of the many habitats of Coyote Lake. In wet areas, **marsh marigolds** show

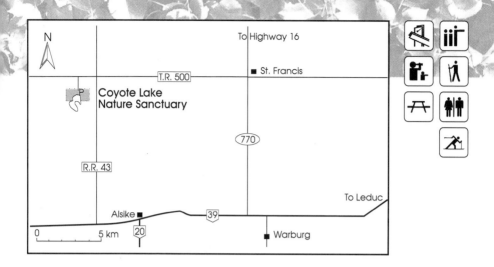

their sunny, yellow blooms and **cotton grass** holds aloft a cottony-white plume. In aspen forest, **common red paintbrush** and **western wood lilies** burn fire-red and orange in the undergrowth. The mauve flowers of **round-leaved orchids** can be seen in low areas among the black spruce.

Stop in during the winter to ski the trails and enjoy the **winter birds** attracted to the feeders at Hopkins' House. Blue jay, gray jay, downy and hairy woodpeckers, white-breasted nuthatches and evening grosbeaks are common visitors.

Common Red Paintbrush

Things to do

- ask your hosts to set up a spotting scope to get a better view of the lake

How to get there

On arrival, proceed to Hopkins' House to register (at a box) and pick up a map/brochure before parking by the picnic area.

For more information, contact:

Doris and Eric Hopkins, Warburg 848-2428

Devonian Botanic Garden
(UNIVERSITY OF ALBERTA)

Location: 5 km north of Devon, 33 km southwest of Edmonton city centre via Hwy. 16 and Hwy. 60
Suggested first-time viewing: 1.5 hours to hike through the tamarack fen
Access restrictions: an admission fee and restricted hours (approximately 10 a.m. to 5 p.m.) in effect from early May to early October. No public access during the winter.

The Devonian Botanic Garden presents a huge variety of plant species from far and wide, including the "Plants of Alberta" collection and the "Native Peoples' Garden." In addition, a 450-ha natural area is connected to the garden facility and leads you through stands of tamarack, birch, poplar and pine.

Tamarack

Special features

The planted gardens include a good selection of plants you're likely to see in the wilds of Alberta. The difference is—they're all labelled! You'll be able to identify **shooting stars, yellow ladies' slippers,** bright orange **western wood lilies** and **blue-eyed grass** at all stages of their development. Be sure to visit in the fall to see them bearing seeds. They often look like different plants altogether and every bit as fascinating.

In the natural area, a boardwalk takes you to the heart of a tamarack fen. What's so special about the **tamarack** (also called larch)? It's the only coniferous tree whose needles turn golden in the fall and drop off, leaving the tree bare over the winter months. Look closely and you'll see how the needles grow in clumps on the branch—a useful field mark. Watch for **boreal chickadees** and **hairy woodpeckers** probing for insects that live in the rough cracks of the bark. The forest floor displays a lush growth of **mosses,** the elegant white flowers of **buckbean** and the spruce-scented **wild black currant**.

What is a **fen**? It is peatland—a poorly drained area where the ground is water-saturated, cool, oxygen-poor and lacking in nutrients. All these characteristics allow a continual build-up of undecomposed plants or peat—also called muskeg.

Downy and Hairy Woodpeckers

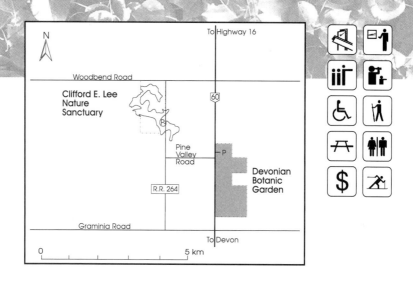

In the tamarack fen and in other wet areas of the site, you'll commonly see **horsetail** (scouring rush). This unusual plant grows up to a metre in height with slender branches growing from joints along the stem. It produces spores—as do mushrooms—to reproduce itself. More than 300 million years ago, the typical horsetail was a tree, growing to 20 m in height. Coal deposits contain the remains of those ancient forests of horsetail.

Things to do

- tour the Butterfly House and Kurimoto Japanese Garden
- join an event or take a course; programs are offered for all age groups

For more information, contact:

Devonian Botanic Garden 987-3054

The Devonian Botanic Garden is operated by the University of Alberta as a research and educational facility.

Scouring Rush

Location: 40 km west of Edmonton city centre
Suggested first-time viewing: 1 hour to walk the 3-km loop trail

At this park, you can enjoy a 3-km walk along the trails combined with a few casts of your fishing line. An enclosed picnic shelter is just the thing to cook up your catch over a crackling fire. Bring some wieners just in case the fish aren't biting! The poplar forest has a dense undergrowth of beaked hazelnut, red-osier dogwood and prickly rose. Around the lake, wet-loving willows and cattails protect nesting birds. Sit quietly along the lakeshore and take in the sights and sounds.

Special features

The 6-cm **brook stickleback** is a fish named for the five or six spines on its back. The male is a conscientious parent, building a nest out of plant stems and defending the eggs until they are hatched. The **threespine stickleback** was illegally introduced to the lake and first noticed in 1980. This invader now competes with native fish and greatly outnumbers the brook stickleback. Get the kids to catch one of these prickly little fish to identify. Be careful not to get jabbed and be sure to return it after getting a close look. It is very important not to transfer any aquatic plants or animals to other water bodies where they may cause unintended harm. (Sticklebacks are best seen in spring when spawning adjacent the floating dock.)

The poplar forest at Hasse Lake is particularly rich in woodland birds. **Ruffed grouse** spend their time on the ground and in the trees searching out buds, seeds and insects to feed on. In the spring, the male attracts a mate by rapidly beating his wings. He sounds like a muffled lawn mower starting up. **Yellow warblers**, sometimes called wild canaries, can be seen flitting through the trees. **White-throated sparrows** regularly sing from hidden places in the dense undergrowth. Their song is a whistled: "Oh, dear Ca-na-da, Ca-na-da, Ca-na-da."

Ruffed Grouse

On the lake, the **ruddy duck** males are the clowns of the waterfowl family with their blue bills, white cheeks and stubby upright tails. As they court the females, they chuck their heads backward and forward and make a sputtering sound with their bills. **American coots**, when alarmed, will usually patter along the surface to get away, rather than taking to the air. Notice how coots bob their

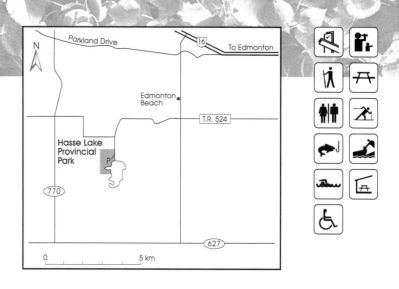

heads back and forth, like a chicken, as they swim. That behaviour has earned them the name "mudhen."

As you walk by open areas along the trails, you'll see little mounds of earth that show no openings. After spring cleaning, the mound-makers plug up the entrance holes to discourage intruders. These mounds indicate burrows that belong to the **northern pocket gopher**, often mistakenly called a "mole." (In fact, there are no moles in Alberta.) Like a mole, however, the pocket gopher is rarely seen. It tunnels down as much as 3 m below the surface, collecting roots to store for winter. Normally, it feeds on green plant material only when it comes to the surface at night.

Things to do

- cast a line from the dock or lakeshore to catch some of the stocked rainbow trout.

- ice-fishing is popular at this lake.

For more information, contact:

Wabamun Lake Provincial Park
892-2702

Ruddy Duck

Location: 14 km northwest of Edmonton city centre on St. Albert Trail
Suggested first-time viewing: 1 hour to walk the short self-guiding trail

Red Willow Park links pockets of nature within St. Albert and a strip of green along the Sturgeon River. Riverlot 56, at the northeast end, is a designated natural area with 16 km of trails winding through poplar woodland and meadow. At the southwest end, Big Lake attracts thousands of birds during spring and fall migrations. In between, cool ravines, river scenes and landscaped grounds are homes to wildlife in every season.

Special features

Follow the change of wildflowers through the seasons at **Riverlot 56**. In spring, **poplar** and **willow catkins** release their white, fluffy seeds, which cover trail edges like a dusting of snow. During summer, bees gather nectar from the bright yellow **goldenrod** blooms. **Saskatoon, raspberry, choke cherry** and **pin cherry** burst with a crop of juicy berries. In the fall, look for the plump, white berries of the **snowberry** shrubs and delicate berries of **star-flowered Solomon's-seal** (neither are good to eat). September brings a blissfully peaceful scene as the sun shines through leaves painted yellow, orange and red. In winter, the woods become even more peaceful as bright red branches of **red-osier dogwood** and frozen red **rosehips** decorate the undergrowth above a blanket of snow.

Red-osier Dogwood

Explore **Red Willow Park** trails along the Sturgeon River for a good view of wildlife in a riparian environment. A 2-km self-guiding trail takes you from landscaped slopes of Colorado blue spruce, under a train trestle dating from the early days of settlement, and through the natural vegetation along the river. River valleys provide important habitat for **mink**. This member of the weasel family patrols the riverbank for mice, fish and the eggs of birds. The younger members of your group may spot, in wet areas, two other favourite meals of this predator: **tiger salamander** (you can't mistake its blotchy patterns) and **wood frog** (with a black mask and white jaw stripe).

Big Lake is a 10-km by 2-km shallow body of water that is almost separated into two parts by an accumulation of soil–a delta–carried in by the Sturgeon River. Waterfowl begin arriving by mid-March and include Canada geese and tundra swans. **Northern pintails** are among the first ducks. These graceful birds with slender necks and long tails migrate from California or the Gulf of Mexico. Notice how they are often already paired by the time they arrive at Big

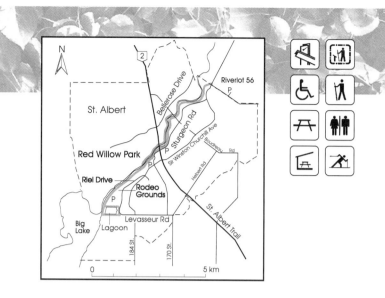

Lake. In your explorations, avoid disturbing any nests you find, since predators such as the **coyote** and **ermine** are more likely to find them once humans have cleared a trail.

Things to do

- pick up a self-guiding trail guide at St. Albert Place. The trail has no stop markers, so follow directions carefully in the guide so you can find the interesting features

How to get there

All the above sites may be reached using the Red Willow Trail system. Pick up a complete map at St. Albert Place.

For more information, contact:

Musée Héritage Museum 459-1528

City of St. Albert, Recreation Services
459-1600

BLESS (Big Lake Environment
Support Society), Box 65053, St.
Albert Centre, St. Albert, Alberta,
T8N 5Y3

Northern Pintail

Suggested guides for more discovery

Natural History Walking Tour (booklet). 1992. Musée Héritage Museum, St. Albert Place, St. Albert, Alberta.

Wabamun Lake

Location: 65 km west of Edmonton city centre
Suggested first-time viewing: 1.5 hours to explore the shoreline adjacent the day
use area at Wabamun Lake Provincial Park

Wabamun Lake is long (20 km), shallow (averages 6.5 m), and is rich in
nutrients, so it produces an abundant crop of aquatic weeds, invertebrates and
fish. Fish-eating birds find this a terrific place to raise their young. The warm
water flushed into the lake from the Wabamun power plant keeps a section of the
lake ice-free during winter, encouraging many birds to stay year-round. You can
get good views of the lake from the wharf at the town of Wabamun, from
Wabamun Lake Provincial Park or from the south side of the lake at Goosequill
Bay.

Special features

The **osprey** is a fish hawk that cruises over the
shallows looking for fish swimming near the surface.
When it spots a fish, it dives straight into the water,
sometimes disappearing from sight and, if
successful, emerges with a fish in its talons.
Ospreys nest in large stick nests high in the trees
or on power poles around the lake.

Common terns have a similar hunting style for
catching minnows. After the young learn to fly,
they can be seen chasing after the parents and
begging for a meal.

The **belted kingfisher** sits on branches
overlooking the shoreline and waits for prey to
appear. Fish, frogs and large insects are favourite
foods. Listen for the loud rattling call, often made in flight.

Osprey

The **great blue heron** relies on stealth, and patience, standing frozen in the
shallows of the lake waiting for prey to come within range. With a sudden thrust
and jab, the heron spears itself a meal. (reedy shorelines)

Fish-eating birds prey on **pike, perch** and **white suckers**. In spring, watch
for these fish spawning (laying eggs) in the shallow water and in streams
entering the lake. **Whitefish** are particularly noticeable during the fall,
spawning in the shallows by the railway trestle where Moonlight Bay joins the
main lake. (Oct.-Nov.)

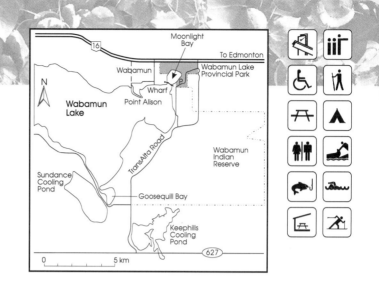

Winter birdwatching may reward you with a sighting of a **bald eagle** or a **gyrfalcon** searching for a meal among the overwintering **mallards** and **common goldeneyes**. Gyrfalcons overwinter at Wabamun Lake before heading back to the Arctic to nest.

Things to do

- at the provincial park, sign out a discovery pack for exploring nature and inquire about educational resource materials for schools and youth groups

- participate in the Wabamun Christmas Bird Count

For more information, contact:

Wabamun Lake Provincial Park, Park Office 892-2702

White Sucker

Wagner Natural Area

July 8/01 Family Adventure c Barney

xx mosquitos

Location: 22 km west of Edmonton city centre on Hwy. 16X
Suggested first-time viewing: 1.5 hours to walk the self-guiding trail

Take your time as you walk this short trail (1.2 km) and explore a natural area packed with fascinating sights, including some very special wild orchids and carnivorous plants. A looped trail and boardwalk take you past soggy fens, marl ponds, willow swamp and muskeg forest of spruce and tamarack.

Special features

Do some plants really eat animals? You bet they do! See if you can spot these seldom-noticed carnivorous plants. They digest insects to gain a nitrogen supplement.

Wood Frog

The **round-leaved sundew** occurs on hummocks of sphagnum moss. When the spoon-shaped leaves with their sticky red hairs trap an insect, they fold over and slowly digest it. Watch for yourself! (flowers July)

Butterworts trap insects in much the same way. The purple flowers resemble a violet and you'll find them growing on the edge of the marl ponds. (flowers June-July)

Bladderworts, which grow in shallow water, extend long stems above the surface to show off bright yellow blooms in July. Attached to the underwater leaves, little bladders open suddenly when stimulated by tiny aquatic animals. The prey is quickly sucked in, where it dies and gives the plant nourishment as it decays.

Watching **toads** and **frogs** is a great family activity. In early May, look for a twin-strand necklace of "black beads" covered in gray jelly (toad eggs) and dark spots in a round mass of jelly (wood frog eggs). In warm weather, the eggs soon hatch into tadpoles: greenish brown tadpoles are **wood frogs**; black tadpoles are **boreal toads**. On spring evenings, listen to the bird-like trill of the male toads calling to the females.

Marl ponds are fed by groundwater springs that are very rich in calcium carbonate, the same white crust that forms around bathroom faucets. When the calcium carbonate settles out, it mixes with peat—dead plants that haven't decomposed in the waterlogged soil—to form the whitish paste called marl. **Stonewort** is an aptly named common plant of the ponds that becomes encrusted with marl and is rough to the touch. Look for a curly **brown moss** growing at the edge of the ponds, named **"fen pasta"** by local students.

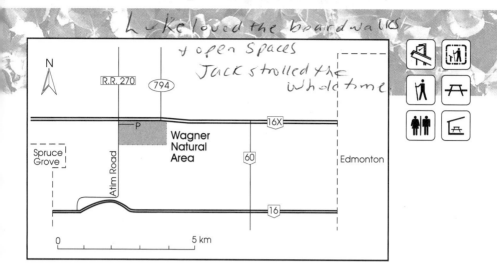

Luke loved the boardwalks + open spaces
Jack strolled the whole time

Marsh marigolds are among the first flowers to bloom in the spring: big, bright and yellow. They are followed by large blue **bog violets** and pink, pointed **shooting stars**. In summer, **western wood lilies**, slender white **asters** and blue **fringed gentians** show their blooms. Mauve flowers of the **round-leaved orchid** appear abundantly in the spruce woods at the north end of the trail in June. It is one of 16 orchid species found at this site.

Shooting Star

Things to do

- join a "Toad Walk" in spring or attend other special events

- wear boots and insect repellent during warm and wet seasons

- stay on the trails since wetlands are very sensitive to trampling

For more information, contact:

Wagner Natural Area Society c/o Heritage Protection and Education Branch 427-5209

The Wagner Natural Area Society is the volunteer steward for the site under the Natural Areas Program. It leases and manages the site for conservation purposes and nature education.

Suggested guides for more discovery

Marl Pond Trail, self-guiding trail booklet, by members of the Wagner Natural Area Society.

East of Edmonton
VIEWING SITES

Site Name	Distance from Edmonton City Centre	Special Features	Page
➊ Beaverhill Lake (Tofield)	67 km E	prime location for watching migrating birds: geese, swans, ducks, shorebirds, bald eagles, hawks, falcons	36
➋ Blackfoot Recreation Area	47 km E	150 km of trails, great blue herons, wapiti, moose, deer, beaver, northern orioles, yellow warblers, double-crested cormorants, American white pelicans	38
➌ Dow Wildlife Greenbelt Viewing Area	35 km NE	Richardson's ground squirrels, Swainson's hawks, nesting waterfowl, common goldeneyes, killdeers, ring-necked pheasants	40
➍ Elk Island National Park	47 km E	103 km of trails, Beaver Hills, high concentration of hoofed mammals: wood bison, wapiti, moose, white-tailed deer	42
➎ Halfmoon Lake Natural Area	54 km N	sandhills, jack pine, bog cranberry, bearberry, reindeer lichen, common nighthawks, cedar waxwings, historic Athabasca Landing	44
➏ Miquelon Lake Provincial Park	70 km SE	beaver, red-necked grebes, aspen, western plains garter snakes, American avocets, snowshoe hares	46
➐ Sherwood Park Natural Area	18 km E	great-horned owls, northern saw-whet owls, pileated woodpeckers, wood frogs, boreal chorus frogs, flowering shrubs, Old Edmonton Trail	48
➑ Strathcona Wilderness Centre	34 km E	black spruce bog, porcupines, red squirrels, red-breasted nuthatches, Labrador tea, sphagnum moss, old man's beard	50
➒ Telford Lake (Leduc)	35 km S	cattails, red-winged blackbirds, marsh wrens, water fleas, migrating ducks and geese, mallards	52

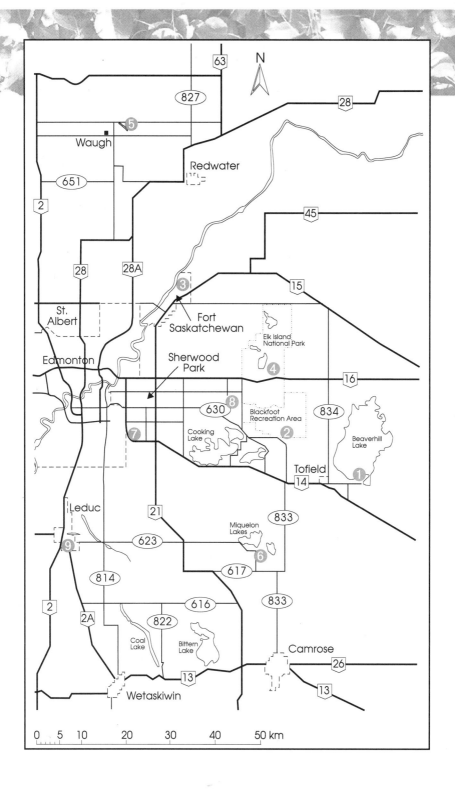

Beaverhill Lake

(TOFIELD)

Location: 67 km east of Edmonton city centre on Hwy. 14
Suggested first-time viewing: 1 hour to explore Francis Viewpoint and the bird
blind, 3 hours to hike the natural area trails.

Imagine looking out over a seemingly endless expanse of water when suddenly
wave upon wave of snow geese fly in formation overhead. Beaverhill Lake is a
Ramsar site–internationally recognized as a special place for migrating birds. It
is a gigantic prairie slough (10 km x 20 km) with inflow during wet periods and
outflow only during high water years.

Special features

Beaverhill is the place to see spectacular numbers of migrating waterfowl and
shorebirds. In spring, these birds head as far north as the High Arctic to breed.
In fall, when they make the return trip, they fly to the southern United States
and even as far as South America.

Listen to **geese** honking loudly as they
fly overhead or rest in the shallow water
along the shore. Locally breeding Canada
geese are the first to arrive – as early as
March 1. Over the next 6-10 weeks
Canada, snow, Ross' and **greater
white-fronted geese** arrive in waves.
Thousands can be seen on any given day

Canada Goose

during the peak of migration. They rest overnight at the lake and, from about
mid-morning till early evening, feed in nearby sloughs and fields.

The more common of our two swan species is the **tundra swan**. It nests in the
far north and overwinters in the United States, passing Beaverhill on its way to
and fro. Watch for these elegant all-white birds, which feed in shallow water
near the shore. The best time to see them is in the fall when some stay until the
lake freezes.

Sandhill cranes give a distinctive musical rattle as they fly overhead during
late April to early May in kilometre-long flocks. They nest in central and
northern Alberta, as well as farther north.

Shorebirds such as the **killdeer** (local nesters) and **dowitchers** (mostly
northern nesters) are attracted to the extensive mudflats and rocky shorelines
around the lake. Over 20 000 shorebirds stop at the lake each year, with
numbers peaking around mid-May and again in mid-August.

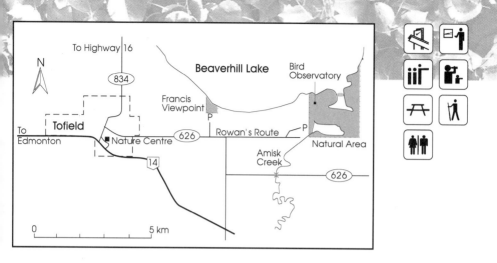

Bald eagles migrate past the lake in spring and fall, often stopping to scavenge dead birds frozen in the ice. Spring is the best time to see up to 18 species of **hawks** and **falcons**.

Things to do

- watch the bird-banding activities in spring or summer at the Beaverhill Bird Observatory
- attend the Snow Goose Festival held during the third weekend in April and the Fall Migration Celebrations on the fourth weekend of September

For successful viewing

- stop in at the Beaverhill Lake Nature Centre
- bring warm clothing and rubber boots since this site can be windy, cold and wet
- bring binoculars and spotting scopes to identify birds at a distance
- caution: roads can be very slippery when wet

Shorebirds

For more information, contact:

Beaverhill Lake Nature Centre, Tofield 662-3191 or Tofield Town Office 662-3269

Beaverhill Bird Observatory, Box 1418, Edmonton T5J 2N5

Suggested guides for more discovery

Prairie Water: Watchable Wildlife at Beaverhills Lake, Alberta. 1991. Dick Dekker, BST Publications, Edmonton, Alberta.

Blackfoot Recreation Area

Location: 47 km east of Edmonton city centre
Suggested first-time viewing: 1 hour to walk the Neon Lake Trail and return by
way of Lost Lake Trail (Waskehegan Staging Area)

Hike into the interior of Blackfoot and you quickly forget how close you are to a
large city. With over 150 km of trails winding through 97 km^2 of rolling
landscape, mostly covered with broadleaf forests and meadows, get set for a real
backcountry experience.

Many different users cooperate to make Blackfoot Recreation Area a success.
Industrial and agricultural uses (natural gas extraction and cattle grazing) take
place alongside hunting, trapping and recreational activities (hiking, horseback-
riding, skiing).

Special features

BLACKFOOT STAGING AREA

Many **great blue herons** nest in a colony
on Blackfoot Lake. The large stick nests sit
high in poplar trees and are most noticeable when
the leaves are off the trees. During the breeding
season (April 15 to July 30), please keep at least
200 m away from the nest colony. (Whitetail Trail)

Great Blue Heron

Blackfoot has enough territory for significant populations
of **wapiti (elk), moose** and **deer**. Listen for bugling
male wapiti challenging each other in the early fall. Look for aspen saplings
rubbed by the males of deer, wapiti and moose as they polish their antlers for the
fall rut. (Buckrun Trail)

CENTRAL STAGING AREA

Well-worn **beaver runs**, leading to water, are common around lakes in the
area. Each active beaver lodge on a lake may house the parents, two or three
young from the previous year and the new kits born in spring. (Beaver Trail)

Birds of the forest make colourful and musical companions. Watch for the
northern oriole and **yellow warbler** as they search for insects in the upper
branches of the aspen trees.

WASKEHEGAN STAGING AREA

Spruce Hollow Trail takes you through a **spruce grove** that survived a fire
that burned through this area in the early 1900s. Spruce forests are shady and
cool in the summer. Lean against a tree and savour the peaceful mood. Look

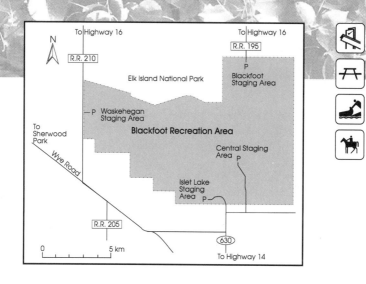

among the spruce needles and **feather mosses** of the ground carpet for bunchberry, twinflower, horsetail and wintergreen.

ISLET LAKE STAGING AREA
The interior lakes of Blackfoot offer secluded places for waterbirds to rest during migration or to nest for the summer. To get a good view of the water, take Lost Lake and Push Lake trails, which follow a ridge around Islet Lake. Look for **double-crested cormorants** and **American white pelicans**.

Wapiti (Elk)

Things to do

- ride a mountain bike or hike into the secluded interior
- plan a picnic at one of the backcountry shelters
- launch a canoe at the boat ramp on Islet Lake

For successful viewing

- pick up a map at any staging area and bring a compass to keep you on the right track

For more information, contact:

Blackfoot Recreation Area Office: 922-3293
Information Line: 922-4676

Dow Wildlife Greenbelt
VIEWING AREA

Location: 35 km northeast of Edmonton city centre; at the northeastern outskirts of Fort Saskatchewan

Suggested first-time viewing: 1 hour to take in the sights at the viewing area

Can wildlife habitat function successfully alongside an industrial site? Come see for yourself. Dow Chemical is making a concerted effort with the development of a greenbelt around its Hydrocarbon Plant. The 8-ha greenbelt reduces the plant's impact by providing habitat for wildlife to raise their young and to use as a movement corridor. At the viewing area, red shale paths lead you across a meadow to a raised platform overlooking marsh and pond.

Special features

Richardson's ground squirrels are Alberta's best known "gopher." Listen for their warning whistles when you get too close, then watch them go scampering down their burrows. They have many different exits to make good their escape, if a weasel should decide to follow them.

Watch for a **Swainson's** or **red-tailed hawk** sitting on a power pole nearby. These common hawks of open areas will swoop down for a meal of ground squirrel, mouse or even grasshopper.

The open waters of specially designed ponds at the public viewing site are fine places to see **nesting waterfowl**. Nesting islands constructed in the ponds provide safe nesting habitat for **shorebirds, ducks** and **geese**. Nesting boxes are placed in trees near the pond for **common goldeneye**. These ducks normally nest in abandoned woodpecker holes. It's amazing how small a cavity can accommodate this duck and its young. After hatching, the young tumble out and follow the female, to be raised among the reeds of the pond.

Red-tailed Hawk

A common shorebird, the **killdeer**, shrieks frantically and feigns injury to distract you from finding its nest or young. The eggs are laid right in the open, on the ground. They are so well camouflaged that one usually finds them only by accident. Hours after hatching, the young begin following their parents, learning to hunt insects.

Killdeer

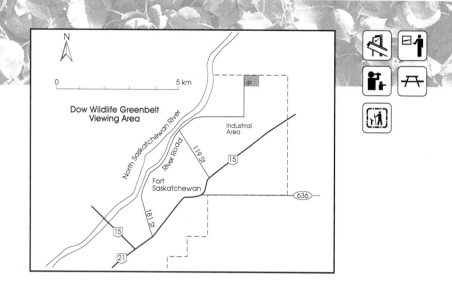

Dow Wildlife Greenbelt
Viewing Area

Ring-necked pheasants are native to southern China and were first introduced into Alberta in 1908. The local fish and game club released them in the greenbelt where fields of sweet clover, blue flax and alfalfa provide food and cover for nesting. The most difficult part of their existence is surviving our winters.

Things to do

- scan the ponds with the spotting telescope provided at the observation platform
- ask about group leader workshops and field trip materials

For more information, contact:

Dow Chemical Canada Inc.   1-800-661-3283

Red Fox

Elk Island

June 23/02   Day Trip   Dean/Lauren/Debbie

Location: 47 km east of Edmonton city centre
Suggested first-time viewing: 1 to 3 hours to view wildlife along the main road
  through the park

Elk Island is part of the Beaver Hills, a rolling landscape probably named for its
large population of beaver so valued during the fur trade era. The diversity of
habitat seen along 103 km of trails attracts a year-round parade of birds
including pelicans and trumpeter swans. However, more than anything else, you
should come here to see moose, deer, wapiti (elk) and bison—representing some
of the highest big game densities in North America.

Special features

Elk Island has one of the highest concentrations of hoofed mammals in the
world.

The **wood bison** is North America's largest native land mammal, weighing up
to 1200 kg. In the mid-1960s, one of only two remaining North American
herds of wood bison was transferred to the park. Today, under careful
management, the species is no longer considered endangered; however, it is still
listed as threatened. Watch the bison graze in the open meadows year-round. In
the spring, rust-coloured calves frolic around their shaggy parents. Look for
wood bison in the area on the south side of Highway 16 and **plains bison** on
the north side. Keep your distance from these animals—bison are dangerous.
(Hayburger Trail, Mud Lake Corral fences at Tawayik Lake Trail, Wood Bison
Trail, Bison Paddock, parkway)

The park was originally established to protect 24 **wapiti (elk)** remaining in the
area. Today, this species is the most common large mammal in the park. In the
fall, listen for the shrill bugling of the bulls, during early morning or at dusk, as
they challenge rivals and court the cows. (Hayburger and Shirley Lake trails)

Moose and **white-tailed deer** browse along
the edges of shrubby or forested areas. Winter is
a great time to see them contrasted against the
white snow and exposed among the leafless
trees. Watch for signs of their activity: cloven-
hoofed tracks, chewed shrubs, droppings, packed-
down grasses and telltale hairs left behind. (Moss
Lake Trail, parkway)

Red-necked Grebe

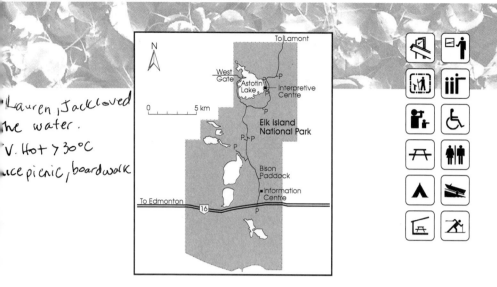

*Lauren, Jack loved
the water.
V. Hot > 30°C
nice picnic, boardwalk*

Things to do

- visit the Astotin Interpretive Centre for displays and information from knowledgeable staff (phone ahead for open hours)
- pond dip for minibeasts at the Living Waters Boardwalk Trail
- please keep your dog on a leash at all times
- drive the 19-km Elk Island Parkway, the Bison Paddock (May–Sept.), and auxiliary roads that lead to Tawayik Lake picnic site/trailhead and to the Warden Office

Coyote

For more information, contact:

Information Centre 992-5790 (summer only)
Astotin Interpretive Centre 992-6392
Warden/Communications Office 992-6380

Elk Island National Park is administered by Parks Canada.

Suggested guides for more discovery

The Discoverer's Guide to Elk Island National Park. 1991. Ross Chapman, Lone Pine Publishing, Edmonton, Alberta.

Finding Birds in Elk Island National Park. 1988. J. Cornish, Friends of Elk Island Society, Fort Saskatchewan, Alberta.

Halfmoon Lake
NATURAL AREA

Location: 54 km north of Edmonton city centre
Suggested first-time viewing: 2 hours to hike to the lake and back

Halfmoon Lake Natural Area overlies rolling sandhills next to the shore of Halfmoon Lake. A trail takes you through open pine forests and dense poplar woods, over grassy meadows, and down into areas of wet muskeg and black spruce. Although the trail to the lake is signed, it is not well-traveled and is somewhat rough.

Special features

Jack pine was considered a bad omen by early settlers because it signified dry, sandy soils where crops tended to fail. It's one of the first trees to sprout after a fire. In fact, the cones don't normally open to expose their winged seeds until they have been scorched. In the undergrowth, look for **bog cranberry, bearberry** (named **kinnikinnick** by Natives) and **reindeer lichen.**

Jack Pine

Some of the jack pines have **dwarf mistletoe** growing on their branches. This parasitic flowering plant causes the pine to develop an abnormal cluster of branches called **witches' brooms.** The fruits of the mistletoe expel seeds to a distance of 10 m. If the seeds lodge in the bark of a tree, a new parasite plant can germinate.

Beginning at dusk, the **common nighthawk** flies aerobatically over the meadows and open pine forest to snap up insects in its large mouth. It's worth an evening trip just to listen to and, on a clear night, to view this bird dive-bombing for insects. Each dive ends with a miniature sonic boom as the nighthawk suddenly sweeps upward.

Cedar waxwings start nesting in July, later than most birds, because the timing must match the development of their food crop–berries. Look for these birds sitting in a row on a wire, gathering in the crown of a tree or feeding in berry bushes. Berry-producing plants flourish at Halfmoon Lake. You'll find **saskatoons, blueberries, raspberries** and **strawberries.** (July–September)

Athabasca Landing Trail is located near the natural area. For information on exploring the trail, go to St. Mary's Church in the village of Waugh. In the late

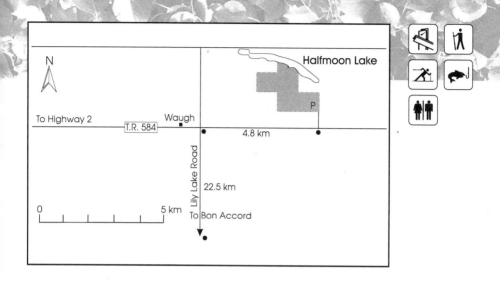

1800s, missionaries, prospectors and others travelled this route. It connected Fort Edmonton, located along the North Saskatchewan River, with the Athabasca River. During the Klondike Gold Rush, it became Alberta's first Dominion Highway.

Things to do

- stay on established trails when exploring this sensitive environment; vegetation is easily disturbed in sandy terrain

For more information, contact:

Heritage Protection and Education Branch, Edmonton 427-5209

Blueberries

Miquelon Lake
PROVINCIAL PARK

Location: 70 km southeast of Edmonton city centre
Suggested first-time viewing: 1/2 hour to walk Grebe Pond Trail and 1.5 hours
to hike the first loop of the Knob and Kettle trails

Miquelon roadways and trails are great places for families to explore for wildlife,
particularly during fall, winter and spring when visitor use is low. This park is
on the southern end and highest point of the Beaver Hills. As you walk the
trails away from the main lake, the ground rises in elevation until you're standing
high on a forested ridge overlooking kettle ponds on either side. Walk further
and you come to the second of the three Miquelon Lakes.

Special features

As you drive into the park, you'll see Grebe Pond just past the permit booth, on
the right side of the road. Park your vehicle in the parking lot a little farther on,
and follow the shoreline trail.

Beaver have built an impressive lodge in the middle of Grebe Pond. The best
time to see active beaver is early morning or late evening. The kids will get a
kick out of hearing the "kerplunk" of a beaver tail as other beaver are warned of
your presence.

Red-necked grebes are easy to spot as they dive for fish and insects in the
open water. With a sharp eye, you might also spot their floating nests anchored
to reeds along the shoreline. (Grebe Pond)

The Knob and Kettle Trail system begins at the baseball diamond. You can hike
an easy 2.5-km loop or go for the whole 8 km, all the way to the second
Miquelon Lake.

Mature **aspens** line the trails. Take a close look at this tree's leaf stalks.
They're flat like an elastic band, causing the leaf to tremble in the slightest
breeze. An old aspen forest has many dead trees, some standing and some
toppled, which provide valuable habitats. Woodpeckers use them for building
nesting cavities, beetles tunnel in the bark and hares scrape out dens underneath
the fallen trees.

Western plains garter snakes like to sun
themselves along trail edges and search for
insects and small frogs around ponds.
Since their skin doesn't stretch, they
shed it, usually in one piece, at regular
intervals of growth.

Garter Snake

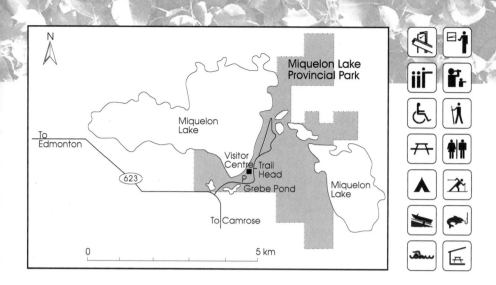

Snowshoe hares make their presence very obvious in winter, leaving tracks, browsed shrubs and droppings throughout the wooded areas. Yet their fur blends in beautifully with their surroundings, by being white in winter and gray-brown in summer.

Things to do

- drop by the Visitor Centre for wildlife displays and activity packs to help you explore for birds, animal tracks and pond life
- attend an interpretive program during the summer months
- rent a paddleboat to navigate the shoreline
- bring the gang out to look for active winter wildlife
- after a winter outing, stoke a fire in one of the enclosed shelters and serve up a snack and hot drink

For more information, contact:

Ranger-in-Charge, Miquelon Lake
Provincial Park, Camrose 672-7274

Suggested guides for more discovery

Summer newspaper and Discovery book
(for children and families), Miquelon
Lake Provincial Park.

Snowshoe Hare

Sherwood Park

NATURAL AREA

Location: 18 km east of Edmonton city centre
Suggested first-time viewing: 1.5 hrs to walk the trail

Walk into this densely wooded natural area and you'll feel as if you're many kilometres away from the city. Some of the forest is over 200 years old, with towering poplar and spruce giving you a sheltered, protected feeling. Here you can ease away everyday worries, and fill your senses with the beauty and wonders of each season.

Sherwood Park Natural Area is a 63-ha wildlife and woodland oasis surrounded by agricultural and residential land. Sitting on the western edge of the Beaver Hills, it's a rolling landscape with poplar and spruce forest, peatlands and swampy areas and a small pond surrounded by marsh.

Special features

Much of this natural area is mature poplar forest—a habitat frequented by owls and woodpeckers.

The **great horned owl** begins nesting early in March, often using the abandoned nest of a hawk. Look for a large twig nest sitting high in a poplar tree and check for the feather "horns" peeking over the edge. If you spot them, a new brood of owlets is on the way. **Northern saw-whet owls** are especially common, nesting in old woodpecker holes. If you're lucky, you might just see a little head poking out of a cavity. The mating call of the saw-whet is heard over and over in the spring, sounding like the high-pitched "beep" of trucks as they back up. The **pileated woodpecker**, a crow-sized and boldly painted bird, chips out large oblong holes near the base of trees looking for carpenter ants and insect larvae. (mature forest)

Great Horned Owl

In the spring, along wet areas of the trail, listen for the "quacking" of **wood frogs**. They are sometimes mistaken for ducks in a flock. The **boreal chorus frog** makes a completely different call, which is like the sound you make running your fingernail along the teeth of a comb. (wet areas or pond)

In the late summer and fall, shrubs that line the lower stretch of trail near the parking lot are laden with fruit: **raspberry, pin cherry, beaked hazelnut, saskatoon, prickly rose, red-osier dogwood** and **choke cherry**. These shrubs provide a food source for wildlife and make a colourful addition to the scenery.

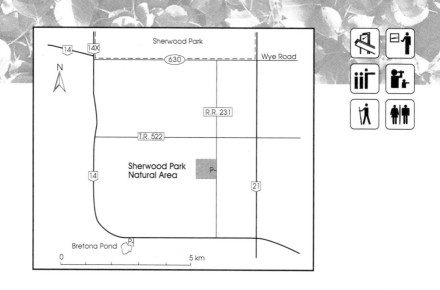

The **Old Edmonton Trail** intersects the hiking trail in a couple of places. Until the 1940s, this road was used heavily by wagon trains moving coal, grain, mine props, lumber, cattle feed and other supplies between the Cooking Lake area and Edmonton. Two of the original survey markers are mounted as plaques for viewing along the hiking trail.

Things to do

- look for interesting bird behaviour from a wildlife-viewing stand at the small pond
- join members of the Strathcona Natural History Club on a guided nature walk
- visit nearby Bretona Pond, just south of Hwy. 14, to watch waterfowl and other marsh birds

For more information, contact:

Strathcona County
Recreation, Parks and Culture
Sherwood Park
467-2211

Beaked Hazelnut

Strathcona

Location: 34 km east of Edmonton city centre
Suggested first-time viewing: 1.5 hours to explore the black spruce bog on Owl Trail

Just a short drive from the city gets you to over 12 km of trails for exploring moose meadows, beaver crossings and Bennett Lake. This publicly operated facility promotes recreation and education in the outdoors but also preserves the environment. A special reason to visit is to explore an easily reached spruce bog. A boardwalk, constructed by the Timber Trekkers troop of the Junior Forest Wardens, takes you right into the midst of this interesting habitat.

*Red-breasted
Nuthatch*

Special features

Take the **Owl Trail** to reach the boardwalk that leads into the black spruce bog. The interior of a spruce forest is well protected from wind, rain and snow by the dense canopy of evergreen needles. **Moose** and **deer** often bed down here during extreme weather conditions. **Porcupines, red squirrels** and birds such as the **red-breasted nuthatch** use this habitat to feed, nest and raise young.

The **black spruce**, with its spindly trunk and irregular limbs, is not your ideal Christmas tree. Look for a club-shaped cluster of dense branches at the top of older trees. This species has an interesting way of reproducing itself. When the lower branches touch the ground and become covered with moss, roots develop and a new tree forms. The cones of the black spruce can withstand the heat of a fire and (like those of jack pine) will open after being scorched.

The floor of the spruce bog is cool and spongy. There is little light and the fallen needles create an acidic soil as they decompose. Only certain plants are able to grow in this environment. Look for **Labrador tea**. It has curled edges on its leathery leaves that persist all year-round. Check the undersides, which are woolly and rust-coloured. The leaves make a strong-flavoured tea.

In the lowest areas, where the forest floor is very wet, you'll find sphagnum or peat moss. Sphagnum acts like a giant sponge, soaking up 20 times its own weight in water.

Black Spruce

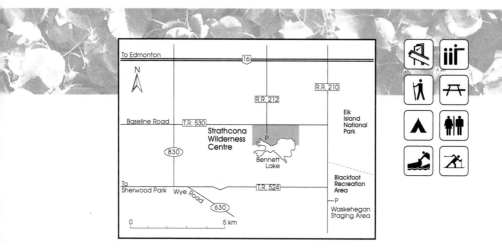

Take a close look to see the intricate detail of this moss.

Old man's beard is a wispy lichen that hangs eerily from the coniferous trees. A lichen consists of two organisms: a fungus and an alga. The fungus provides a home for the alga, which by itself converts sunlight into food. Together, they form a winning team.

Things to do

- register for an exciting range of outdoor education programs for individuals, families or groups in every season
- book the lodge as a retreat for your group
- rent skis, snowshoes and canoes at reasonable prices.

Note: fees are charged for facility bookings and ski trail passes.

For more information, contact:

Strathcona Wilderness Centre 922-3939

Labrador Tea

Telford Lake
(LEDUC)

Location: 35 km south of Edmonton city centre, at the east side of Leduc
Suggested first-time viewing: 1.5 hours to walk the lakeshore trail

Who would think that right on the edge of residential Leduc, there sits a haven for aquatic wildlife? Stroll down the long boardwalk to get a clear view of the lake. A 5-km asphalt trail skirts the lake edge, weaving past willows, aspen woods and lakeshore vegetation. Along the way, lean on the railing of an observation platform, read the interpretive signs and enjoy the sights. Wildlife species are partial to lake edges, so you'll find lots of birds and water critters here.

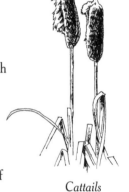

Special features

Cattails are the first thing you'll notice as you approach the lake. As soon as you see their hotdog-shaped seed heads, you know you're about to enter marsh habitat. The leaves of the cattail are used by birds to build nests and by **muskrats** to build lodges. Muskrats also eat marsh vegetation, including the leaves of the **arrowhead** plant, which is rooted in the mud at the lake edge and produces attractive white flowers, some of which become clusters of green fruit.

Cattails

You'll likely spot the male **red-winged blackbird** straight away, as he shows his stuff, balancing on top of a cattail. Now, look carefully for a **marsh wren**. Since they spend most of their lives hidden in the reeds, these wrens can be difficult to spot. But you are likely to hear the male's song – a loud rattle coming from within the reeds. The marsh wren builds a round nest woven into the supporting stems of marsh plants, with an entrance on the side. The male will often build a few dummy nests to confuse predators.

Scoop up a handful of the lake water and look closely for **tiny animal life**. These minibeasts are food for larger insects, fish, frogs, snakes and waterfowl. Look closer still and you should be able to see the beating of a large oval heart through the transparent outer shell of a **water flea**.

Red-winged Blackbird

It makes good sense to preserve Telford Lake when you see the hundreds of **ducks** and **geese** that stop here

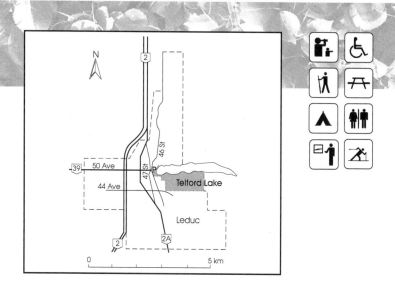

during spring and fall migrations. In spring plumage, the male **mallard** sports a glossy green head, white collar and chestnut breast. Later in the summer, the feathers begin to moult and the male then resembles the female with its mottled brown colour. During this moulting period, most ducks are unable to fly and must stay in deep water or hide in the reeds to escape predators.

Things to do

- visit the Wood's House Museum for an audiotape tour of life during the Roaring Twenties. It's just a block west on 49th Ave.

- campers at Leduc Lions Campground in southeast Leduc can travel along the trail system to Telford Lake.

For more information, contact:

City of Leduc, Community Services
980-7116 or
Alberta Fish and Wildlife District Office,
Leduc 986-6775

Water Strider

Wabamun Lake-Lac Ste. Anne
AUTO TOUR

Distance: 100 km round trip from Wabamun Lake Provincial Park
Driving time with no stops: 2 hours

This scenic drive takes you alongside three large lakes west of Edmonton. In between, you'll drive a landscape with a mix of rolling farmland and poplar and spruce forest. This tour starts and ends at Wabamun Lake Provincial Park, but you can also start the tour from Edmonton via Highways 16 or 16X, or Hwy. 627. An Edmonton starting-point will add about 125 km (1.5 hours) to the tour.

Stop #1 – Wabamun Lake Provincial Park

The exit from Hwy. 16 to the park is well-marked as you approach from the east. The access to the park is on your right a short distance south of the highway. Scan Moonlight Bay or go for a short hike along park trails. Check page 30 for detailed information.

Stop #2 – Wabamun Town Dock

Return to Hwy. 16, travel a few kilometres further west and turn south at the highway marker to the Wabamun Town site. Stop at the parking and day use area near the dock.
Scan the large marsh between the dock and Point Alison. The water from the Wabamun power plant keeps this part of the lake open year-round. Look for **eagles** on the larger trees on Point Alison (winter).

Common Merganser

Stop #3 – The Narrows

Return to Hwy. 16 and cross the highway going north past the Whitewood mine to the Narrows on Lac Ste. Anne (17.8 km). Watch for **ospreys** on towers along the power line. The Narrows, which joins the two parts of Lac Ste. Anne, is a favourite fishing spot for both anglers and **waterbirds** such as grebes.

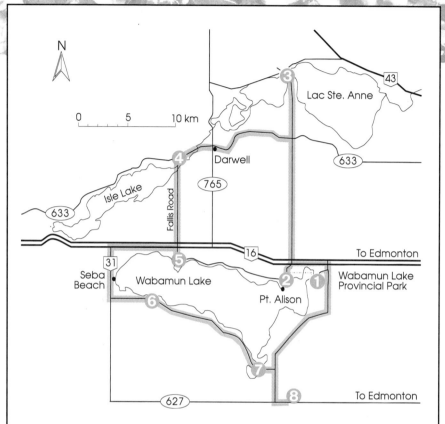

Wabamun Lake - Lac Ste. Anne Auto Tour

1 - Wabamun Lake Provincial Park

2 - Wabamun Town Dock

3 - The Narrows

4 - Isle Lake

5 - Fallis

6 - Wabamun Natural Area

7 - Goosequill Bay and Power Plant

8 - Keephills Cooling Pond

Northern Pike

Stop #4 – Isle Lake

Backtrack south to Hwy. 633 and turn west. Drive
9 km west to the Fallis Road (3.2 km past the
community of Darwell), then turn south and within
1 km you will pass over a bridge at the east end of
Isle Lake. You can stop here at Baybridge Park,
which has picnic tables and pit toilets. This part of
Isle Lake is shallow and marshy and there are usually
lots of waterbirds visible from the road. You may be
lucky enough to see **gray jays** near the picnic
site–looking for scraps of leftover food. Isle Lake forms
a part of the headwaters of the Sturgeon River, which
flows into Lac Ste. Anne, Big Lake and eventually the
North Saskatchewan River near Fort Saskatchewan.
Continue south on the Fallis Road to Hwy. 16.

Gray Jay

Stop #5 – Fallis

Continue south across Hwy. 16 at Fallis and onto a hill overlooking Wabamun
Lake's Coal Point. There is a wide spot to pull off near the top of the hill. You
can see the Sundance and Keephills Power Plants and the mine across the lake.
Look for **ospreys** on the artificial nest platform visible near the spruce trees on
the west side of Coal Point. (At this point the route can be shortened by
following the north shore road eastward, back to the Wabamun townsite.
Continue east down the hill and along the lakeshore. Watch for ospreys along
the north shore of the lake. An exposure of brick-red shale occurs on the north
side of the road, the result of a burnt-out coal seam.)

Stop #6 – Wabamun Natural Area

Return to Fallis at Hwy. 16, turn west and drive to the Seba Beach turnoff at
Hwy. 31. Head south past Seba Beach, then east on Sundance Road to the
Wabamun Natural Area (4.0 km from the corner). This site is at a higher
elevation than the lake and so it attracts different plants and animals than seen
along the shore. The natural area has no facilities and is not well-marked, but it
is definitely worth a short stop.

Stop #7 – Goosequill Bay and Power Plant

Follow the road past the Sundance Power Plant to Goosequill Bay. This large
shallow marsh usually has numerous birds. The cooling pond behind the dyke to
the southwest of the road is a good spot to view **overwintering waterfowl**.

Stop #8 – Keephills Cooling Pond

Continue farther east to a T-intersection, then turn right to get to Keephills Cooling Pond. You can return to Edmonton via Hwy. 627, or else backtrack north and go through the Wabamun Indian Reserve to the provincial park and Hwy. 16. If you follow Hwy. 627, note the deep valley of Wabamun Creek, with its growth of spruce forest. You will also get a good view of the North Saskatchewan River Valley near the site of an early fur-trading post, Upper White Mud House.

Spotted Sandpiper

Cooking Lake Moraine

AUTO TOUR

Distance: 110 km round trip from southeast city limits
Driving time with no stops: 2.2 hours

The Cooking Lake Moraine makes for an interesting drive on roads that wind over hills and into hollows of this hummocky landscape. About 10 000 years ago, huge blocks of ice encrusted with silt, sand and gravel broke off from melting glaciers. As these buried blocks of ice melted, they left hills and hollows, which are now forested ridges and water bodies.

Stop #1 – Sherwood Park Natural Area

Leave Edmonton via Sherwood Park Freeway and drive to Range Road 231 on the east side of Sherwood Park. Turn right and drive south 4 km to the natural area. Stop in the parking lot on your right. Glance over the interpretive trailhead signs for an overview. If you're intrigued, and time allows, walk the trail of this heavily wooded site. It lies on the western edge of the Cooking Lake Moraine. Check page 48 for detailed information.

Stop #2 – Bretona Pond

Continue 2.5 km farther south on Rge. Rd. 231 and then 3 km west on Hwy. 14. Turn south at the Watchable Wildlife sign, then turn right into a parking area. This site is Bretona Pond–a Buck for Wildlife habitat development site. A short walk will take you to the floating dock and viewing area. Most waterfowl will stay on the west side of the pond, so a pair of binoculars will come in handy. Scan for **eared grebes, black terns, tree swallows** and **red-winged blackbirds**.

Black Tern

When you leave Bretona Pond, drive 14 km east on Hwy. 14. Be on the lookout for bird boxes on fence posts along the highway. Tree swallows and **mountain bluebirds** use these boxes for raising young.

Stop #3 – South Cooking Lake

Turn left into town and follow the day use picnic table signs to South Cooking Lake Park. Walk down to the lake and look for waterfowl, eared grebes, **canvasbacks, ring-necked ducks** and **Canada geese**. **Bald eagles** pass through in spring and fall.

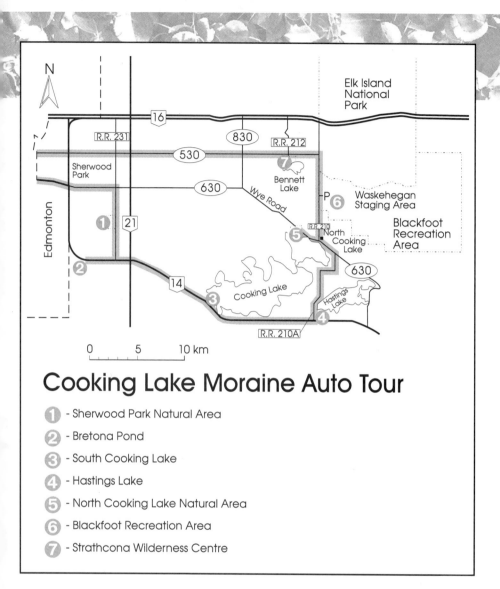

Cooking Lake Moraine Auto Tour

1 - Sherwood Park Natural Area

2 - Bretona Pond

3 - South Cooking Lake

4 - Hastings Lake

5 - North Cooking Lake Natural Area

6 - Blackfoot Recreation Area

7 - Strathcona Wilderness Centre

When you get back to the highway, turn left and continue east. You'll cross a marsh, which is a shallow bay of Cooking Lake. Watch for Canada geese and the exotic-looking **yellow-headed blackbird**. The road then curves left around the lake. Take the moose-crossing sign seriously because there are plenty of **moose** and **white-tailed deer** in the area. You will then be driving through the middle of the Cooking Lake Moraine and will notice many ponds along the road. Most contain waterfowl and some of the larger ponds have a beaver lodge.

Stop #4 – Hastings Lake

After driving 13 km, turn left at the Deville sign onto Range Road 210A. Within 2 km, you'll see Hastings Lake on your right where there is room to pull off the road. The west end of the lake is shallow and attracts lots of waterfowl. **American white pelicans**, terns and **double-crested cormorants** use this lake for fishing. **Western grebes** nest in a colony in the off-shore reed beds.

American White Pelican

Stop #5 – North Cooking Lake Natural Area

Continue north on this road for about 4 km through the ranching country between Cooking and Hastings lakes. Continue to Hwy. 630 and follow it to the west. About 3.5 km past the hamlet of North Cooking Lake there is a natural area parking lot on your left. (Note: parking lot is at intersection of Twp. Rd. 522 and Hwy. 630.) If you feel energetic, hike the wetlands trail to the shore of Cooking Lake (about 1 hour). Wear good hiking or rubber boots since the trail is rough and often wet. The trail traces more than 1.5 km of shoreline, with aspen forest, ponds, meadows and wetlands along the way. In June, July and August, look for the world's smallest flowering plant–ducksmeal. It resembles green grains floating on the water's surface. Puddle ducks like **mallards** and **blue-winged teal** scoop these plants from the water.

If you're running out of time, head back to Edmonton on Wye Road (Secondary Hwy. 630).

Stop #6 – Blackfoot Recreation Area

Drive back to the hamlet of North Cooking Lake and turn north on Range Road 210. Drive 4.6 km, watch for the signs and turn right into the Waskehegan Staging Area. You could stop here for a meal at the picnic shelter–or stretch your legs on a trail. Check page 38 for detailed information, or stop at the park office for current brochures.

Stop #7 – Strathcona Wilderness Centre

Continue driving north on Range Road 210 along the west fence line of the Blackfoot Recreation Area, which then becomes the boundary of Elk Island National Park. Look for **wood bison** that frequently graze along this fence line.

Don't get out of your vehicle to approach the bison; they may charge at you. After 4 km, turn west along Baseline Road (Twp. Rd. 530). After about 3 km, look for signs and a large gate entrance leading from the south side of the road and into the Strathcona Wilderness Centre. Check in at the centre to enquire about events. Check page 50 for detailed information.

To return to Edmonton, continue west on Baseline Road for about 30 km.

Mountain Bluebird

Gwynne Outlet

AUTO TOUR

Distance: 190 km (round trip from south city limits)
Driving time with no stops: 2.5 hours or less

During the time that glaciers covered much of Alberta, some ice and debris blocked the flow of water from melting glaciers, damming a huge lake that covered the Edmonton area. The water broke through the ice-dam and escaped to the south in a raging flood. In a matter of days, the water scoured a valley, as much as 50 m deep and 1 km wide, now called the Gwynne Outlet. Saunders, Ord and Coal lakes still hold water in the valley of this ancient meltwater spillway.

Eared Grebe

Stop #1 – Telford Lake

Drive 16 km south of Edmonton on Hwy. 2 to Leduc. Take the Calmar/Drayton Valley exit and turn east to Leduc centre. Follow 50th Ave. over the railway tracks, turn right on 46th Street, then immediately left into the Telford House parking lot. Telford Lake is a side channel of the Gwynne Outlet. Get a good view of the lake from the boardwalk. Watch for **red-necked grebes, gadwalls, ring-necked ducks, Canada geese, blue-winged teals, ruddy ducks** and **eared grebes**. Check page 52 for detailed information.

Stop #2 – Saunders Lake

Go back on 50th Ave. to 50th St. and turn south to Hwy. 623. Turn east and drive to the south end of Saunders Lake, about 7 km. Park near the top of the hill on Range Road 243. Be careful of traffic as you walk down the hill. This lake lies in the Gwynne Outlet channel. As far as you can see, this valley extends north and south. Imagine how it looked about 12 000 years ago, when the outlet carried a thousand times the water flow of the North Saskatchewan River.

Stop #3 – Coal Lake, north end

Upon leaving Saunders Lake, drive east 1 km past farmland and rolling hills. Turn south on Hwy. 814 and drive 13 km. Then turn east on Hwy. 616 and

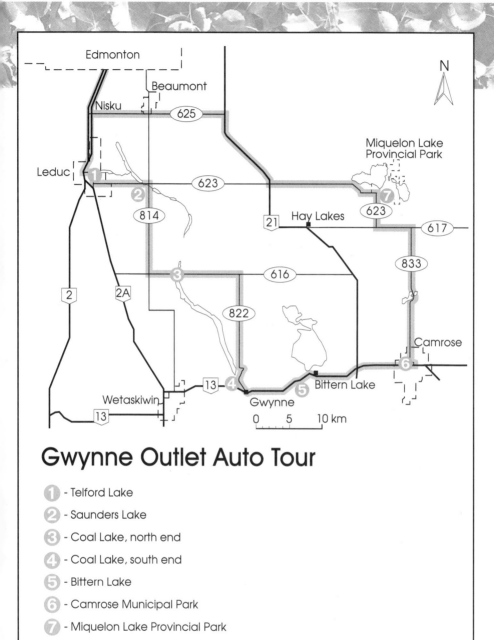

Gwynne Outlet Auto Tour

1 - Telford Lake

2 - Saunders Lake

3 - Coal Lake, north end

4 - Coal Lake, south end

5 - Bittern Lake

6 - Camrose Municipal Park

7 - Miquelon Lake Provincial Park

drive about 4 km. The large valley ahead is the Gwynne Outlet again, with Coal Lake nestled in the bottom. Drive down to a provincial campground in the valley bottom. The lake has good fishing for **yellow perch** and **northern pike**. You can also expect to see fish-eating birds such as **terns, cormorants** and **pelicans**. If the kids have energy to burn, explore the trails and woods that border this narrow lake.

Stop #4 – Coal Lake, south end

Follow Hwy. 616 to the east, up and out of the valley, and drive just over 8 km to Hwy. 822. Set your odometer, since Hwy. 822 is not marked. Look for hawks such as the **Swainson's hawk** sitting on fence posts. Also watch for ducks and shorebirds at several wetlands along this road. Turn south on Range Road 230 (Hwy. 822) and drive 15 km to another campground at the south end of Coal Lake. A dam across this end of the lake controls the water level. Look for **common goldeneye** and other ducks.

Lesser Yellowlegs

Stop #5 – Bittern Lake

Travel a couple more kilometres south and you hit Hwy. 13. Turn east toward Bittern Lake. As you leave the Gwynne Outlet channel, you pass the town of Gwynne on the south side of the road. After 8 km, watch for the Bittern Lake Campsite to the south. Look for **shorebirds** and **waterfowl** on the alkaline wetlands around the campsite. Bittern Lake itself is difficult to reach, but you can get a good (though distant) view of the lake from the first road to the north, about 1 km east of the campground.

Stop #6 – Camrose Municipal Park

Follow Hwy. 13 east for 13 km to Camrose. Just a few blocks into town, you'll see an Information Centre on the north side of the road, which is adjacent Mirror Lake. Stop to view the displays and get current information. Walk the trails leading from the centre and look for the **trumpeter swans** that are kept in the park year-round. These birds were used to breed some of the trumpeter swans re-introduced into Elk Island National Park.

Stop #7 – Miquelon Lake Provincial Park

Turn north on 51st Street just past Mirror Lake and then go west to 53rd Street. Follow that street north where it becomes Hwy. 833. About 7 km out of town, the road angles around several sloughs. Check for **waterfowl** activity. Another 9 km will bring you to Hwy. 617. Turn west and travel 5 km to Hwy. 623; turn north and continue about 5 km along the road to Miquelon Lake. Park just past the permit booth on the right side of the road. A short paved trail

follows the shoreline of Grebe Pond. A large **beaver lodge** sits smack in the centre of the pond and **red-necked grebes** are never far from view. Check page 46 for detailed information.

Follow Hwy. 623 west from Miquelon Lake Provincial Park to Hwy. 21 and turn north. When you reach Hwy. 625, turn west and drive 20 km to Hwy. 2. After you pass Beaumont and just before Nisku, you'll drive through a wide, shallow valley. This valley is your farewell view of the Gwynne Outlet. Continue to Nisku, then north on Hwy. 2 to Edmonton.

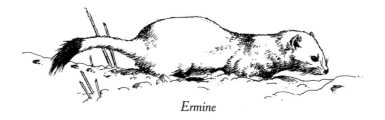

Ermine

Sources for Further Information

Agency and Organization Contacts

The following agencies and organizations are knowledgeable sources of information, including site-specific natural history information.

Alberta Environmental Protection, Information Centre, Main Floor, 9920-108 Street, Edmonton, T5K 2M4. Ph. 944-0313

Alberta Fish and Game Association, 6924-104 Street, Edmonton, T6H 2L7. Ph. 437-2342

Beaverhill Lake Nature Centre, Town of Tofield, Box 30, Tofield, T0B 4J0. Ph. 662-3191

Edmonton Bird Club, Box 1111, Edmonton, T5J 2M1.

Edmonton Geological Society, c/o Dept. of Geology, University of Alberta, Edmonton, T6G 2E3.

Edmonton Natural History Club, Box 1582, Edmonton, T5J 2N9.

Elk Island National Park, Site 4, R.R. #1, Fort Saskatchewan, T8L 2N7. Ph. 992-6380

Federation of Alberta Naturalists, Box 1472, Edmonton, T5J 2N5. Ph. 453-8629

Heritage Protection and Education Branch (Natural Areas Program), Alberta Environmental Protection. Ph. 427-5209

Natural Resources Service, Fish and Wildlife Edmonton Metro Office. Ph. 427-3574

Provincial Museum of Alberta, 12845-102 Avenue, Edmonton, T5N 0M6. Ph. 453-9144

The City of Edmonton, John Janzen Nature Centre, P.O. Box 2359, Edmonton, T5J 2R7. Ph. 496-2939

The City of Edmonton, River Valley Outdoor Centre. Ph. 496-7275

Editor's Choice of References

The following publications provide basic information about various aspects of natural history of wildlife and plants, including identification. From here, the sky is the limit! Each of these publications contains additional reference titles, which will allow you to understand better the interesting behavioural and ecological observations you make during your visits to wildlife-viewing sites in and around Edmonton.

Unless otherwise indicated, these references are available in bookstores as well as libraries.

GENERAL NATURAL HISTORY:

Alberta Naturalist – quarterly publication of the Federation of Alberta Naturalists (see Contacts on p.66), available through the organization or libraries for back issues; natural history research and information; news about meetings, conferences and local affiliated clubs' activities.

Edmonton Naturalist – periodical publication of the Edmonton Natural History Club (see Contacts on p.66), available through the organization or libraries for back issues; natural history of plants and animals in the Edmonton area; news about meetings, and field activities.

Knee High Nature in Alberta – Winter 1988, (Fall 1989, Summer 1990, Spring 1991) – D. Hayley and P. Wishart. Knee High Nature, Sherwood Park; children-oriented books told simply, well-illustrated with drawings; focused on bringing children and parents together while doing activities.

ANIMALS:

Alberta Mammals: An Atlas and Guide. 1993. H.C. Smith. The Provincial Museum of Alberta, Edmonton; brief descriptions of distribution, habitat and key identifying features of Alberta's 91 species of mammals; plots distribution on provincial-scale maps; skull drawings and measurements for the serious student of mammals; photographs.

Little Brown Bat

Hoofed Mammals of Alberta. 1993. J.B. Stelfox (ed.). Lone Pine Publishing, Edmonton; comprehensive reference to Alberta's nine species of ungulates; includes identification based on tracks, skulls, scats, antlers and horns; reviews ecology, physiology, management; photographs.

The Atlas of Breeding Birds of Alberta. 1992. Federation of Alberta Naturalists, Edmonton; covers Alberta's 270 breeding birds, including their distribution,

habitat and nesting preferences; detailed provincial-scale map of breeding records; photographs.

Birds of Edmonton. 1990. (revised). R. Bovey, Lone Pine Publishing, Edmonton; an introduction to Edmonton's more common species of birds; illustrations for identification of these species; discusses bird feeders, attracting birds, nest boxes and backyard habitat.

Birds of North America. 1983. C.S. Robbins, B. Bruun and H.S. Zim. Western Publishing Company, Inc., Racine, Wisconsin; identifies more than 650 species from North America north of Mexico; shows plumage differences and song patterns; small-scale seasonal distribution maps; illustrations.

Field Guide to the Birds of North America. 1987. (second edition). National Geographic Society, Washington, D.C.; includes over 800 species that occur in North America; describes physical features, breeding habitats and seasonal distribution; small-scale maps; illustrations.

The Amphibians and Reptiles of Alberta. 1993. A.P. Russell and A.M. Bauer. University of Alberta Press, Edmonton, Alberta; detailed physical descriptions, natural history and distribution information; for each species, provincial-scale maps feature site records; photographs.

Fishes of Alberta. 1992. (second edition). J.S. Nelson and M.J. Paetz. The University of Alberta Press, Edmonton, Alberta; all 59 species of fish known to occur in Alberta are described; natural history and distribution are detailed; provincial-scale maps with site records along watercourses and in water bodies; discusses management and taxonomy; photographs.

Butterflies of Alberta. 1993. J.H. Acorn. Lone Pine Publishing, Edmonton; detailed physical descriptions of butterflies occurring in Alberta; natural history information; focused on viewing of butterflies; photographs.

PLANTS:

Canadian Tiger Swallowtail

Flora of Alberta. 1983. E.H. Moss. (second edition revised by J.G. Packer.) University of Toronto Press, Toronto; technical keys and descriptions of all ferns, fern allies and flowering plants known to occur in Alberta, apart from more recent records; distribution maps; for the more serious student of botany.

Mosses, Lichens & Ferns of Northwest North American. 1988. D.H. Vitt, J.E. Marsh and R.B. Bovey. Lone Pine Publishing, Edmonton; photographic field

guide; distribution maps; ecological habitat guide; identification keys; general description.

Mushrooms of Western Canada. 1991. H.M.E. Schalkwijk-Barendsen. Lone Pine Publishing, Edmonton; illustrated identification guide; species descriptions; assessment of edibility.

Trees and Shrubs of Alberta. 1990. K. Wilkinson, Lone Pine Publishing, Edmonton, Alberta; detailed physical descriptions of 77 species; keys for identification; small-scale maps of distribution in province; photographs.

Western Canada Violet

Wildflowers Across the Prairies. 1984. F.R. Vance, J.R. Jowsey and J.S. McLean. Western Producer Prairie Books, Saskatoon, Saskatchewan; nontechnical field guide to nearly 400 species of flowering plants; color photos and blackline sketches.

Wildflowers of Alberta. 1977. R.G.H. Cormack, Hurtig Publishers Ltd., Edmonton, Alberta; brief physical descriptions for identification of about 400 species of the more common wildflowers in Alberta; distribution is described; general information and uses discussed; photographs.

VIEWING SITES:

Alberta Wildlife Viewing Guide. 1990. Alberta Forestry, Lands and Wildlife and Lone Pine Publishing, Edmonton; more than 60 wildlife-viewing sites are described; features information on access, seasonal viewing, key species and viewing practices; photographs.

A Nature Guide to Alberta. 1980. Prov. Museum of Alberta Publication #5, Hurtig Publishers Ltd., Edmonton; describes wildlife and other natural features for 171 viewing locations in the province; information on access; regional maps with sites indicated; viewing ethics; photographs.

Alberta's Natural Areas: A Guide to Selected Sites. 1991. Alberta Forestry, Lands and Wildlife, Edmonton; a guide to 32 of Alberta's most interesting and well-established natural areas; location maps plus information on natural features and facilities.

Edmonton Beneath Our Feet. 1993. J.D. Godfrey (ed.). Edmonton Geological Society, Edmonton (see Contacts on p.66); reviews basic geology of landforms, geological history, fossils, groundwater and soils of Edmonton area; discusses economic and practical aspects of geology; detailed viewing guide for geological features of North Saskatchewan River Valley trail.

Notes

Notes

Notes